IMMERSION
Bible Studies

1 & 2 TIMOTHY, TITUS, PHILEMON

Praise for IMMERSION

"IMMERSION BIBLE STUDIES is a godsend for participants who desire sound Bible study yet feel they do not have large amounts of time for study and preparation. IMMERSION is concise. It is brief but covers the material well and leads participants to apply the Bible to life. IMMERSION is a wonderful resource for today's church."

Larry R. Baird, senior pastor of Trinity Grand Island United Methodist Church

"This beautiful series helps readers become fluent in the words and thoughts of God, for purposes of illumination, strength building, and developing a closer walk with the One who loves us so."

Laurie Beth Jones, author of *Jesus, CEO* and *The Path*

"The IMMERSION BIBLE STUDIES series is no less than a game changer. It ignites the purpose and power of Scripture by showing us how to do more than just know God or love God; it gives us the tools to love like God as well."

Shane Stanford, author of *You Can't Do Everything . . . So Do Something*

IMMERSION
Bible Studies

1 & 2 TIMOTHY, TITUS, PHILEMON

James Earl Massey

Abingdon Press

Nashville

1 & 2 TIMOTHY, TITUS, PHILEMON
IMMERSION BIBLE STUDIES
by James Earl Massey

Copyright © 2012 by Abingdon Press

Library of Congress Cataloging-in-Publication Data
Massey, James Earl.
  1 & 2 Timothy, Titus, Philemon / James Earl Massey.
    pages cm — (Immersion Bible studies)
  ISBN 978-1-4267-0990-6 (curriculum—printed / text plus-cover : alk. paper) 1. Bible. N.T. Timothy—Textbooks. 2. Bible. N.T. Titus—Textbooks. 3. Bible. N.T. Philemon—Textbooks. I. Title. II. Title: First & Second Timothy, Titus, Philemon.
  BS2745.55.M325 2012
  227'.806—dc23
                                                                              2012005333

Editor: Jack A. Keller, Jr.
Leader Guide Writer: Martha Bettis Gee
12 13 14 15 16 17 18 19 20 21—10 9 8 7 6 5 4 3 2 1

Manufactured in the United States of America

Contents

Review Team

Diane Blum
Pastor
East End United Methodist Church
Nashville, Tennessee

Susan Cox
Pastor
McMurry United Methodist Church
Claycomo, Missouri

Margaret Ann Crain
Professor of Christian Education
Garrett-Evangelical Theological Seminary
Evanston, Illinois

Nan Duerling
Curriculum Writer and Editor
Cambridge, Maryland

Paul Escamilla
Pastor and Writer
St. John's United Methodist Church
Austin, Texas

James Hawkins
Pastor and Writer
Smyrna, Delaware

Andrew Johnson
Professor of New Testament
Nazarene Theological Seminary
Kansas City, Missouri

Snehlata Patel
Pastor
Woodrow United Methodist Church
Staten Island, New York

Emerson B. Powery
Professor of New Testament
Messiah College
Grantham, Pennsylvania

Clayton Smith
Pastoral Staff
Church of the Resurrection
Leawood, Kansas

Harold Washington
Professor of Hebrew Bible
Saint Paul School of Theology
Kansas City, Missouri

Carol Wehrheim
Curriculum Writer and Editor
Princeton, New Jersey

IMMERSION BIBLE STUDIES

A fresh new look at the Bible, from beginning to end,
and what it means in your life.

Welcome to IMMERSION!

We've asked some of the leading Bible scholars, teachers, and pastors to help us with a new kind of Bible study. IMMERSION remains true to Scripture but always asks, "Where are you in your life? What do you struggle with? What makes you rejoice?" Then it helps you read the Scriptures to discover their deep, abiding truths. IMMERSION is about God and God's Word, and it is also about you—not just your thoughts, but your feelings and your faith.

In each study you will prayerfully read the Scripture and reflect on it. Then you will engage it in three ways:

Claim Your Story
> Through stories and questions, think about your life, with its struggles and joys.

Enter the Bible Story
> Explore Scripture and consider what God is saying to you.

Live the Story
> Reflect on what you have discovered, and put it into practice in your life.

IMMERSION makes use of an exciting new translation of Scripture, the Common English Bible (CEB). The CEB and IMMERSION BIBLE STUDIES will offer adults:

- the emotional expectation to find the love of God
- the rational expectation to find the knowledge of God
- reliable, genuine, and credible power to transform lives
- clarity of language

Whether you are using the Common English Bible or another translation, IMMERSION BIBLE STUDIES will offer a refreshing plunge into God's Word, your life, and your life with God.

1.

On Being Responsible

1 Timothy 1:1–3:16

Claim Your Story

What chores were assigned to you while you were growing up? What memories come to mind? In addition to being assigned some task, you were probably admonished to be timely—and agreeable—in handling that task. In youthful rebellion most of us sometimes chafed at handling some duties, but later in life we look back on it all with appreciation for the lessons early labor taught us, grateful for the trust and approval we received from managing things properly.

Our parents or guardians wisely introduced us to responsibility; they guided us in what was to be done, teaching us how to be responsible. Handling those chores helped us become responsible adults.

As I read through memoirs and biographies, I am always alert for storied information about how persons learned to be responsible, which helps me better understand what followed as a result. We all appreciate stories about successful persons, and much of that appreciation has to do with how their stories underscore the importance of being committed, honoring trust, being responsible.

John Hope Franklin, the noted historian, has told in print about how his parents instilled self-reliance and a sense of responsibility in him and his sisters when they were growing up in Rentiesville, Oklahoma. "[We] had duties," Franklin stated. "I had to clean the lamp, chimneys, and fill them with kerosene. We had no electricity. And my sister and I had to get in the wood. The wood was chopped, but it was outside. We had to bring the wood in the house. . . . That's the way kids were raised in those days. You obeyed. Something to do, you did it. We had a real sense of hard work and industry instilled in us."[1]

The first letter of Paul to Timothy was written to encourage the young church leader to maintain a responsible ministry and to train others for responsible living and labors. The letter treats the themes of trustworthiness, attentiveness to doctrine, godliness, and devotion to duty.

Enter the Bible Story

Concerning Timothy the Man

Timothy, to whom the letter is addressed, worked very closely with Paul. His name is linked with Paul's in many of the apostle's letters to churches (2 Corinthians 1:1; Philippians 1:1; Colossians 1:1; 1 Thessalonians 1:1; 2 Thessalonians 1:1), and his activities are referred to in many of those letters as well. Paul lauded Timothy in the Letter to the Philippians as "like-minded" (2:20, NKJV) with him and trustworthy, and reported proudly that "as a son with a father" Timothy had served with him in ministry (2:22, NKJV). At the time this first letter was sent to Timothy, he was on a mission in Ephesus, handling an assignment entrusted to him by the apostle, who had mentored him for ministry.

Acts 16:1-3 gives us a brief biographical sketch of Timothy. He was a native of Lystra (in Galatia) and the son of a mixed marriage; his mother was Jewish and his father was Greek. During Paul's first ministry in Lystra (see Acts 14:6-20), mother and son were converted; when Paul returned there about two years later he was so impressed by reports about their development in faith and their standing within the Christian fellowship that he invited Timothy to accompany him in ministry (Acts 16:3). Having been reared by his mother as a Jew, Timothy had been taught the Scriptures (see 2 Timothy 3:14-15). Paul recognized Timothy's spiritual growth and giftedness and helped the young man learn and appreciate the duties and disciplines of ministry as they worked in tandem: Paul leading, Timothy assisting. Timothy served with Paul in Thessalonica (1 Thessalonians 3:5), Corinth (1 Corinthians 4:17), Philippi, Troas, and Miletus, as well as during Paul's lengthy and dramatic preaching and teaching stay in Ephesus. Working with Paul, and learning from him, Timothy developed leadership skills and faithfully managed assignments whenever and wherever the apostle deemed it fitting. Thus those affectionate words of greeting as the first letter opens: "To Timothy, my true child in the faith" (1 Timothy 1:2).

Timothy's Task Restated

Timothy was instructed to be intentional and decisive in teaching the believers under his charge. Perhaps prone to be modest in manner, Timothy was encouraged to review his task and manage it seriously and courageously like a soldier engaged in warfare with "these instructions . . . if you follow them, you can wage a good war" (1:18).

First of all, Timothy is to combat wrong teaching and false teachers, teachings and teachers that deal more with ethnic lore and esoteric subjects—which stir controversy—rather than with truths that promote godliness. "The goal of instruction is love from a pure heart, a good conscience, and a sincere faith," Paul states (1:5). Important to this end, then, is "sound teaching" (1:11), namely, doctrine based on the gospel.

Some of the people had also been distracted from the truths of the gospel through inept teachings regarding "the Law" (see 1:6-8). From the very first decade of the church's life, questions were raised regarding the role of the Mosaic law in Christian life. Both those of Hebrew background and those from the Gentile world had an interest in the answer, but few leaders were sufficiently informed to settle the debate. Paul knew that some would-be teachers in the church were teaching the law "without understanding either what they are saying or what they are talking about with such confidence" (1:7). Unlike Paul, they did not have a right view regarding the law; they could not properly distinguish between its ceremonial strictures and its moral principles, they did not know what had been abolished through the sacrificial death of Jesus and what remains as moral demand, what was preparatory and what continues as permanent. Paul does not dwell on the matter, however; he simply states that law, divine or otherwise, "is good if used appropriately" (1:8).

About the Scripture

Authorship of the Pastoral Epistles

First and Second Timothy and Titus all bear the name of Paul the apostle as their source, a fact that accounts in part for their eventual acceptance in the New Testament canon, the collection of books recognized by the church as Scripture. But biblical scholars over the past 150 years have not agreed about whether Paul was *directly* or *indirectly* that source.

The traditional view attributes the letters directly to Paul, assuming that he penned or dictated them late in his life, which would date them to the 60s of the first century. A corollary of this view is the assumption that Paul had a "second career," not recorded in the Book of Acts, after a first imprisonment in Rome and that Paul returned to the Aegean instead of pursuing his earlier plan to go to Spain. Not only do the letters explicitly claim to have been written by Paul, scholars supporting the traditional view point out that there was universal acceptance in the early church (beginning at least by A.D. 200) of the letters as written by Paul himself. Further, the strikingly personal character of several passages in the letters, particularly 2 Timothy 4:6-21 and Titus 3:12-13, is taken by some scholars as compelling evidence of Paul's direct authorship.

Pseudonymous writing was not uncommon in the ancient world; it was seen as a means of extending a "living tradition" as authoritative. Many scholars are persuaded that there are good reasons to conclude that the Pastorals were not written by Paul himself but by his close followers a generation later who wrote in Paul's name to represent the heritage received from their great founding apostle in the face of later challenges. If that is the case, these letters would date to the late 80s or 90s of the first century.

There are several reasons that many scholars think that Paul did not write the Pastoral Letters. For instance, the distinctive vocabulary and the writing style of these three letters differ from Paul's other letters. Also, the degree of church structure or organization is more developed here than in Paul's undisputed writings. Further, the Pastorals seem to reflect greater accommodation with the norms and structures of Roman society, especially household order, than elsewhere in Paul's correspondence.

Neither side in the scholarly dispute about authorship denies that First and Second Timothy and Titus are all related to Paul *in some way*. The church has accepted these books, along with the undisputed letters of Paul, as Scripture, as inspired by God and useful for building up the community of believers. It is important, therefore, that we as twenty-first-century Christians not let the issue of authorship prevent us from listening carefully to what God may be saying to us today in the Pastoral Letters.

Paul's Testimonial Thanksgiving

Paul's critique of inept teachers of the law, and the vice-list of sins committed by those who live contrary to divine law (see 1:9-10), perhaps triggered memories about his earlier zeal for the law and how that zeal had caused him to misjudge Jesus and persecute him and his followers in the name of the law. If his rather long testimonial thanksgiving in 1 Timothy 1:12-17 to Christ Jesus for saving and entrusting him to preach the gospel is understood in this light, then it will not seem out of place in this section where he has treated "wrong teaching." The fact that he had earlier been dead wrong in his zealous war against Christians must surely have been on his mind as he thought about how the law has been mishandled. He must have realized, as well, that his testimony could hearten Timothy, because it would help the young leader better appreciate being trusted with the gospel.

In Paul's testimonial thanksgiving about what issued from Christ to grant Paul his new life and calling, four words stand out boldly: *mercy, favor, faithfulness,* and *love* (1:13-14). Remembering how with blasphemy he had spoken slanderously against Jesus, how with unbridled zeal he had arrested followers of Jesus, and how he was "in full agreement" with the murder of Stephen (see Acts 8:1), Paul knew his past was not only sordid but sinful. Although his past made him consider himself as "the biggest sinner of all," Paul knew that the mercy, grace, faith, and love he had experienced in submitting himself to Christ left all that past behind. Paul was a changed person, with a new life, a new status, a new record, a new role. The testimonial thanksgiving that appears here in this letter is from a grace-claimed man whose heart knew at deep levels that God's grace is efficient, sufficient, and abundant. And he was determined to be responsible in spreading the word about that grace. "This saying is reliable and deserves full acceptance: 'Christ Jesus came into the world to save sinners'" (1 Timothy 1:15). That was and remains the central message of the Christian faith, and every believer's change of life validates its truthfulness. Small wonder, then, that Paul, grace-influenced, broke into praise as he closed out his testimony, exulting: "Now to the king of the ages, to the immortal, invisible, and only God, may honor and glory be given to him forever and always! Amen" (1:17).

Congregational Prayer

In addition to establishing central doctrine, Timothy is instructed to establish a meaningful prayer tradition (2:1-8). In stating "First of all," as he begins this section of the letter, Paul wants it understood that the subject about to be mentioned is one of several he will treat, but also that it is of primary importance. That first subject is *congregational prayer*.

Paul encourages different kinds of prayers in the congregation. He mentions "requests," because the church should make entreaties to God for divine help. He mentions "prayers," probably as an inclusive term for group devotions and customary invocations. He mentions "petitions," the meaning of which is readily clear. Next, Paul mentions "thanksgivings," grateful praise to God for God's sensed presence, answered entreaties, and merciful deeds.

But Paul went further: he urged that congregational prayers should be offered for more than the assembled members, that prayer should be made on behalf of "all people" (2:1). Prayer is personal, yes; and particular, yes; but it is not to be parochial or partial.

Paul then mentions the need to pray for civic leaders. There is more here than a healthy respect for a government system; there is also voiced here a basic understanding that a peaceful public order is important for human safety, for promotion of the general welfare of all, and, in that particular setting, for having a "quiet and peaceful life in complete godliness and dignity" (2:2). Paul recognizes that "this is good" (2:3, KJV and NIV) and pleases God, who wants everyone to hear and accept the gospel.

Paul's instructions about congregational prayer for public order are sometimes neglected in the church, due perhaps to a preoccupation on our part with individual needs. But the neglect is also due to a widespread misunderstanding of how important prayer can be in influencing the direction of civic decisions. Prayer is part of a Christian's response to life and a necessary means for communion with God. Given what Paul has advised here about the practice of prayer within the congregational meeting, we should understand congregational prayers as part of our Christian work in the world, as a way to effect change in the world. Please note that prayer is only *part* of our work, but perhaps it grants the most creative edge to our work in the world. While there are all-too-many times when we believers seem thwarted where public influence is concerned, times when we are made to know that a biblical vision for the human order will not be allowed, yet believers must stay open in faith and prayer, planning what to do while waiting, and watching for openings to press the case for our Lord. As a Christian response to life, prayer is a creative and influencing deed. In any and every event, prayer is strategic, even if it only seems to shape us to confront an erring social order.

The goal of a safe and progressive public order should remain a concern in the prayers of a church. If a church is so busy with other interests that the public good is neglected, then an ill-advised religious focus will have sidetracked the group, blinding its members to the fact that to separate the faith from common life in the world is to work against God "who wants all people to be saved and to come to a knowledge of the truth" (2:4).

In stating the case as he did, that God "wants all people to be saved," Paul was not making a case for universalism; he was only stating that the gospel is of universal scope, that salvation is intended for all who will respond to what God offers openly in Christ. "There is one God and one mediator between God and humanity, the human Christ Jesus, who gave himself as a payment to set all people free" (2:5-6a).

Paul cautioned that prayer, whatever its category—request, petition, or thanksgiving—is valid only when the praying person's attitudes and actions do not block fellowship. There must be no "anger or argument" separating that person from others. Christians are not to use prayer as a

---

Across the Testaments

There Is One God

First Timothy 2:5-6, which quotes an early Christian creed, begins with the affirmation that "there is one God." We see here clear evidence that the early Christian community reaffirmed the monotheism of the central creedal claim of Judaism (the Shema; see Deuteronomy 6:4-9), in sharp contrast to the polytheism of the surrounding Roman culture.

factional weapon, praying *at* one another instead of *to* God or praying for a narrow party line instead of for God's will for the whole church.

Personal Attire and Decorum During Worship

Paul advised that, when the church gathered, its members should not dress ostentatiously or engage in gender competitiveness. No gender struggles in the home between a wife and husband were to be allowed to affect the peaceful purpose of the group. Paul's strictures addressed to the women (wives?) and his explicitly stated preference for male leadership within the gathering—"I don't allow a wife to teach or to control her husband. Instead, she should be a quiet listener" (2:12)—might be best understood as part of his concern about the deleterious effects on gender relations caused by the worship of the goddess Diana, a prevalent fertility cult in Ephesus. Luke's report in Acts 19:23-41 about Paul's earlier encounter with devotees of that entrenched religious cult sheds some light on this matter.

Although Paul's exact words tend to shock us initially as apparently patriarchal bias, his ruling here should be understood as addressed to a specific context and not as an absolute rule to be universally observed. Passages in Paul's other letters appear to grant women both dignity and freedom in the life and work of the church. One such obvious passage is Galatians 3:28. Another is 1 Corinthians 11:5, where both prayer and prophesying by a woman would be activities where speech on her part would be public. The problem of Paul's wording continues to be debated, but one thing is clear: his "I don't allow..." at 1 Timothy 2:12, seems distinctly individual in tone, not something that is divinely sanctioned as an absolute principle to be universally applied.

Congregational Governance

Paul moves next to the subject of *congregational governance* (3:1-16). Drawing on a second "reliable saying" within the church, Paul affirms the importance of supervision in the congregation's life and applauds personal ambition to serve in that role: "If anyone has a goal to be a *supervisor* in the church, they want a good thing" (3:1, emphasis added). In reading the term "supervisor" ("bishop," NKJV, NRSV; "overseer," NIV), our thinking is initially influenced by our knowledge about the later development of hierarchical ecclesiastical orders in the church. But there is nothing hierarchical in the collegial structure Paul describes here for the church (or cluster of house-congregations) Timothy was sent to help. Paul had in view the practical need for a chief leader among the believers, such as existed in Jewish synagogues, and he went on to list the personal qualities needed by anyone eager to fill and manage that role. As stated in 1 Timothy 3:2-7, the person who would be appointed as "supervisor" must be disciplined, faithfully married, well-behaved, sober-minded, dignified, hospitable, gifted to teach, not given to drink, not greedy for gain, and must possess good management skills for handling household matters and family relations. Furthermore, that person should have a good name in the wider community.

The "supervisor" would need to be aided by other persons qualified to serve as needed. Paul designates such aides as "servants" (3:8, 10, 12-13, CEB; "deacons," NKJV, NRSV). The personal qualities he lists for such "servants" are similar to those required for the congregation's "supervisor." The "supervisor" and "servants" were charged with helping the congregation handle its responsible work in the world.

As Paul thought further about the church, its members, and its origin and strategic mission as "the church of the living God and the backbone and support of the truth" (3:15), he reflected anew about the greatness of the Christ whose life forms the center of that truth. Paul quotes a celebrative hymn as he marvels to Timothy in 3:16 about the Christ they serve. "He was revealed as a human"—he had a real life like ours. He was "declared righteous by the Spirit"—meaning God vindicated him by raising him from death after he was crucified. He was "seen by angels"—seriously observed and studied by them as he went about his saving mission. He was "preached throughout the nations" and "believed in around the world"—rightly so, because of his universal and eternal importance. And he was "taken up in glory"—from whence he shall return to consummate history and gather the full fruit from his sacrificial and saving deed.

Live the Story

Yes! "Without question, the mystery of godliness is great" (3:16a). All who comprise the church are responsible to be active "managers of God's secrets" (1 Corinthians 4:1), and it is required of managers that they prove themselves responsible and faithful. Having ascended, and presently seated at God's right hand, Jesus will have the last word about all things. Meanwhile, we who look to him as Savior and obey him as Lord must continue to live responsibly.

No word is more central for our self-understanding and fulfillment than this one: *responsibility*. We were created to be responsible persons, and when converted we were recreated in Christ to act with accountability to the truth—the truth as it is in Jesus. We are responsible for following the course truth lays out before us, sharing our witness about the Savior and sharing ourselves in service in the world around us. Paul the apostle lived such a life, witnessing across the Roman Empire about Jesus as Savior. Faithfully responsible, as he urged Timothy to be, Paul made an indelible imprint in history and on Christian life and thought.

The world of our time awaits *our* witness and necessary work!

> Let us, then, be up and doing,
> With a heart for any fate;
> Still achieving, still pursuing,
> Learn to labor and to wait.[2]

How are *you* being responsible? How does your life witness to Christ? What are you doing to share yourself in service to God and neighbor? What next steps might God be calling you to take?

1. See the interview with John Hope Franklin in *The Word: Black Writers Talk About the Transformative Power of Reading and Writing: Interviews*, edited, and with an Introduction by Marita Golden (New York: Broadway Paperbacks, 2011), 142, 143.

2. Henry Wadsworth Longfellow, from "A Psalm of Life," *The Complete Poetical Works of Henry Wadsworth Longfellow* (Boston: Houghton, Mifflin and Co., 1893), 3.

2.

Maintaining Community Order

1 Timothy 4:1–6:21

Claim Your Story

If you were asked what you think about when you hear the word *church*, what would you likely mention? Would you find yourself speaking initially about a treasured building where you gather to worship? Would you mention religious services? Would you find yourself talking about a particular circle of people with whom you share a pilgrimage in grace? Or would you speak about a customary weekly experience when traditional ceremonies are honored and observed? Just how do you understand, regard, and define *church*?

If you were asked to assess the health and face-the-world readiness of the denomination or church to which you belong, what criteria would you use to do so? What, to you, are signs and evidence of a vital church life?

These are important questions we must be prepared to answer in our postmodern era. They are important initially because they prod those of us who are connected with the church to go behind secondary meanings we associate with that word, however precious those meanings may be, to discover or recover the basic biblical meaning of what the church is, why it is, and how it came to be.

As a manual of teachings that address these issues, First Timothy restates and celebrates the touchstones of Christian faith and offers guidelines to establish and maintain church faith and church order. Paul reminds us that church life, rightly understood, is associated with something other than static institutionalism, social prominence, and ritual that has become empty. Rather, church life has to do with people who engage in living by, protecting, and passing on Christian truth, with an interest in the salvation of all people (1 Timothy 2:4). Such a people, and such activities, Paul teaches in this letter, are the primary signs of life in the church.

Enter the Bible Story

Challenges to Church Order

Church life is never simple and seldom is it static; "happenings" constantly take place. As the faith is taught, the expected "happening" within some believers is a desire for clarified thinking, increased understanding, and disciplined living. Sharing the faith beyond the fellowship results in new conversions, and the congregation rejoices over the gain.

Like every meaningful society, the church extends itself by two means: one, by the addition of new participants, as new converts are added to the ranks; and second, through training its members to exemplify core Christian values. These meaningful "happenings" have the power to motivate believers, to mobilize them for inspired service to God and others.

But sometimes there are "happenings" of another kind, happenings that block rather than bless the church mission. People bring with them into the fellowship a range of learnings and likings, some of which can cause group friction, and even worse, spawn factions. Thus Paul's Spirit-prompted warning that "some people will turn away from the faith" (1 Timothy 4:1), led away by deceptive teachings inspired by Satan. Although having turned from the faith, they do not always leave the group. They pretend to show the same interest in belonging as before, but for selfish reasons. Such people put on a false show of piety, but their inner lives are marred by hearts that are not pure. Questioning what they earlier accepted as the truth, they later renounce what they once embraced.

Such persons will be selfishly ambitious, Paul warns. Overzealous to excel in piety, their asceticism will spur them to prohibit marriage and even to forbid the eating of many foods that God created for human consumption (4:3). Paul warned that their asceticism is based on spiritual deception, and he encouraged Timothy to combat their erroneous views by teaching about the goodness of God's creation, and about the efficacy of the prayer-blessing usually offered before eating food.

Across the Testaments

Everything Created by God Is Good

To counter the false teachings of those who advocated an ascetic lifestyle, Paul insists that "everything that has been created by God is good" and should be received with thanksgiving (1 Timothy 4:4). The echo with the creation story in Genesis 1:1–2:4 is unmistakable. Everything that God has created is "good," even "very good."

Training in Godliness

Timothy was also charged to illustrate true piety and virtue to the people by his life and labors (4:7b-16). Like a success-minded athlete, he was to train himself in godliness, laboring to show that his commitment to God was total. He was told that godliness develops by training and that, though young, he could model that godliness through his "speech, behavior, love, faith, and by being sexually pure" (4:12). Help is found, Timothy is told, in being attentive to the reading of Scripture during gatherings of the church; in the practice of preaching the Scriptures; and by remembering his call and rehearsing anew the prophetic words the elders spoke to and about him when, along with Paul, they laid their hands on him. Paul assured Timothy that practicing these things would bear fruit for himself and for those to whom he had been sent (see 1 Timothy 4:13-16).

Youth and Age

Paul concerned himself earlier with gender differences and the crises they can engender in the church (2:8-15), but mindful too about how generational differences can affect relationships, he advises Timothy about how these should be managed (5:1-2). Seniors, male or female, are to be treated respectfully and never sharply rebuked. They are to be respected like one's natural father or mother. In the same spirit of familial regard, the young men and young women in the church are to be regarded and treated like one's brothers and sisters.

The reasons Paul included instructions on handling generational differences are readily apparent. Youth and age differ in experience, in perceptions, interests, social roles, responsibilities, opinions, in overall view of things, and even in feelings about things. Then as now, generational differences can occasion conflict between youth and older adults. One of the duties of a church leader is to manage conflict wisely, always working to help members relate and work as family. Both church order and essential ministry depend upon wise leaders who can help members of all ages learn to be partners in mind and spirit.

Care for Widows

In 1 Timothy 5:3-16, Paul addresses the subject of caring for a particular category of widows in the church. Women members who are to be considered eligible for church support must be those whose husbands have died; they must be sixty years old or older and have no estate benefits or grown children to support them; and they must not have remarried. Such a widow must be "truly needy," must have a record of faithfulness as a wife, and "a reputation for doing good: raising children, providing hospitality to strangers" and other deeds of dedicated service (5:10). Paul's basic principle here is twofold. One, family is supposed to be a network of supportive relationships. Two, when the family network is unable to help those persons who are needy, the church has a responsibility to help.

Across the Testaments

Compassion for the Poor and Vulnerable

The many stipulations in deuteronomic law (for example, Deuteronomy 10:18; 14:29; 24:19; 27:19) and injunctions in the prophetic literature (see Isaiah 1:17, 23) show that a tradition of compassion and social service to the needy had long been the standard for Israel. Paul instructed the church to continue that tradition of care. This caring impulse at the heart of the Judeo-Christian tradition helped influence the establishment of a social security system for the elderly, the indigent, and orphaned children in many nations in the Western world.

Elders

In 1 Timothy 5:17-25, Paul returns to the subject of leadership (which he treated in 3:1-13) and here explains the rights of the "supervisors" and "servants"—here considered together as "elders"—as they handle their responsibilities in the church. "Elders who lead well should be paid double, especially those who work with public speaking and teaching" (5:17). The words "paid double" might be construed to mean just that, but the concern Paul expresses here is really twofold: those who lead well deserve and should receive both "honor" (5:17, NIV and NRSV) and support (5:18). The honor they deserve includes the benefit of a full and fair treatment if accused concerning any matter (5:19); the accusation is not to be considered except in the presence of two or more persons qualified to hear and judge its merits, an injunction that follows Deuteronomy 19:15 (and the near-parallel teaching of Jesus in Matthew 18:16). But any elder who openly sins, that is, "in front of everyone" (1 Timothy 5:20), must be disciplined. The statement actually commands that a public rebuke occur, so that all other members and leaders will feel the shamefulness associated with wrongdoing.

In no instance must bias be allowed or favor shown to persons who are popular (5:21). There must be no rush to appoint, commission, or install anyone, so that no wrong person is positioned in a role for which they are not morally and experientially equipped. An appropriate period should be allotted to examine any potential leader's background and lifestyle before entrusting certain roles to them. To place a person who habitually sins in such a position, Paul warns, is to participate in the sins of others" (5:22). He goes on to say that "the sins of some people are obvious" while "the sins of other people show up later" (5:24).

In the midst of his instructions about elders, Paul advised Timothy about a way to help himself better manage an apparently frequent stomach problem: "Don't drink water anymore but use a little wine because of your stomach problems and your frequent illnesses" (5:23). As part of his regimen to avoid becoming addicted to wine, Timothy probably was drinking only water. Paul advised that he not totally abstain, like an ascetic, but that he should use a little wine occasionally for his gastric problems.

Whether Paul meant some grape juice in its fermented state or the freshly pressed juice from grapes, mixed with water, is not clear. What is clear, however, is that "little" is a term denoting quantity. Following Paul's advice, Timothy could thus take care of his health, avoid playing into the hands of extreme ascetics who were troubling the church, and also remain free from addiction to alcohol (see 1 Timothy 3:3).

Slaves

Paul instructs slaves who are members in the church to give their masters full respect. We read those words and wince. Paul's tacit acceptance of a system that kept persons "under the bondage of slavery" as something to be protected shocks us, remembering, as many of us do, that a brutal slavery system once existed here in America, and that the sad heritage from that system still plagues our national life. Paul's advice here to Christian slaves that they "should consider their own masters as worthy of full respect" is initially offensive. Even the reason he cites for the advice seems to rob the individual of dignity: "so that God's name and our teaching won't get a bad reputation" (6:1).

One need only read the narratives of former slaves to get an inside look into the horrors suffered under the bondage of slavery and to understand why the instruction Paul voiced to slaves seems insensitive. One such slave narrative came from the pen of Frederick Douglass.[1] Born about 1817, Frederick Douglass was the son of a black slave and her white owner; his mother died in his sixth year of life in bondage. Blessed with ambition, intelligence, and the will to be free, Frederick escaped to the North. Helped by white abolitionists, he began a new life as a free man in New Bedford, Massachusetts, in 1838. Douglass taught himself to read and write, and went on to become one of this nation's most accomplished orators, a major leader among abolitionists, a chief spokesman for African Americans, and one of the ablest critics of churches in America that allowed and endorsed slave-holding.

Writing in 1845 as a Christian believer and a minister in the A.M.E. Zion Church, Frederick Douglass said about the slave-holding churches of the South:

"I am filled with unutterable loathing when I contemplate the religious pomp and show, together with the horrible inconsistencies, which every where surround me. We have men-stealers for ministers, women-whippers for missionaries, and cradle-plunderers for church members.... He who proclaims it a religious duty to read the Bible denies me the right of learning to read the name of the God who made me. He who is a religious advocate of marriage robs whole millions of its sacred influence, and leaves them to the ravages of wholesale pollution. The warm defender of the sacredness of the family relation is the same that scatters whole families,—sundering husbands and wives, parents and children, sisters and brothers,—leaving the hut vacant, and the hearth desolate."[2]

"The over-whelming mass of professed Christians in America," Douglas continued, "strain at a gnat, and swallow a camel.... They would be shocked at the proposition of fellowshipping a sheep-stealer; and at the same time they hug to their communion a man-stealer, and brand me with being an infidel, if I find fault with them for it."[3]

Paul admitted that slavery placed persons under bondage, but he made no frontal attack against the system. Although there were many inequities within the way the Roman Empire ordered its affairs, Paul evidently accepted that way and sought to work creatively within it. Paul was acquainted with slaves, and he regarded them as persons in their own right; he knew that enhancing their personal growth in godliness could help them be even more influential within the master's household, and that their respect and loyalty toward a master—especially a master who was also a Christian—could help gain concessions, perhaps access to some personal holdings, and even the prize of freedom for services rendered. Since the master/slave relation was part of the way the Roman Empire ordered its life and affairs, Paul tailored his advice to Christian slaves to help them manage their bondage creatively. While this explanation does not excuse Paul's apparent acceptance of slavery, it does help explain his approach in dealing with it. He urged Christian slaves to respect their masters so that the church's teachings would not be viewed as a threat to the social stability of the secular order. Paul reasoned that if the church moved directly against the expected order of things it would be viewed as a seditious group, be classified as an illicit religion, and lose the freedom it had to evangelize.

Interestingly, Paul, a free person and a Roman citizen, sometimes in his writings referred to himself as a "slave of Jesus Christ" (Romans 1:1; Philippians 1:1; Titus 1:1). Did he use this designation strictly to show his loyal subservience to Jesus the Lord, or did he also use it to openly identify himself with slaves in the ordered households he often visited? We ask, but cannot know. Paul wanted to be known as someone in the service of a Master; he wanted it known that he had been "bought with a price" (1 Corinthians 6:20, NRSV) and that all things concerning him were subject to his Master's will. It is not incidental that the term *slave* is one of the most used legal images in the writings of the apostle Paul.[4]

Moneyed Members

Some of the members of the church at Ephesus were affluent, or were eagerly working to improve their financial standing. In 1 Timothy 6:5-19, Paul addressed the moneyed members in the church. He advised them to be sensible and balanced in the way they thought about wealth and in the way they dealt with it. Those with money were not to think that their wealth was evidence that they were godly, and they were warned against trying to use religion as "a way to make money" (6:5). Those with money were not to "become egotistical and not to place their hope on their finances" (6:17). They were told to be sensible about what they possessed and to remember that "we [humans] didn't bring anything into the world and so we can't take anything out of it" (6:7). They were warned that craving wealth can become a poisoning passion that leads to "all kinds of evil" (6:10), that a fixation on financial gain can cause one to sin by an overweening pride, a consuming greed, a stingy spirit, an extravagant lifestyle, and a self-inflicted anxiety. These troubles can be avoided if, instead of selfishly craving wealth, one pursues "righteousness, holy living, faithfulness, love, endurance, and gentleness" (6:11), while maintaining "hope in God, who richly provides everything for our enjoyment" (6:17b).

Wealth need not be greedily hoarded and selfishly handled. Wealth can be meaningfully gained and rightly used. Wealth can help sustain a household, undergird a business enterprise and employees, and aid philanthropic causes. The moneyed members were thus told to "do good, to be rich in the good things they do, to be generous, and to share with others" (6:18). The generosity and sharing could support church ministries, compensate the leaders, and provide care for the needy widows.

Live the Story

The church is an intricate mosaic of persons, brought together in a definite tradition of teaching that is rooted in the revelation of God in Jesus Christ. All who belong to the church are charged with an assignment to spread the word that "Christ Jesus came into the world to save sinners" (1:15). We must handle our task together, each member and leader serving our Lord in "love from a pure heart, a good conscience, and a sincere faith" (1:5). We serve best when there is a shared regard for each other, when we are responsible in our judgment, and when there is no selfish concern for personal gain or control.

We must understand ourselves as more than a voluntary association and something other than a fraternity, sorority, or club. We are "God's household" (3:15), an ordered family of believers whose reason for being has to do with more than ourselves; it has something to do with "all people." We serve a God who earnestly wants everyone "to be saved and to come to a knowledge of the truth" (2:3). Basic to being relevant as "the church of the living God" is faithfulness in teaching, and living out, preserving, and passing on the faith. The core subject-matter of the faith remains the same through changing times and passing generations. And the basic norms for maintaining church order have not changed. We have a mission to accomplish, a mission that requires our faithfulness, support, and togetherness.

The church is a spiritual community not yet perfected. It is even now still in process, facing new challenges and demands and the temptations that lie along the path. What are the patterns of leadership in *your* church? What aspects of Paul's letter to Timothy does *your* congregation especially need to hear? What aspects of the letter trouble you? What evidence of vital church life do you see around you? What is the central message of faith that your congregation embodies, protects, and communicates to others?

1. *Narrative of the Life of Frederick Douglass: An American Slave, Written by Himself* (New York: Penguin Group, 1968 reprint of 1845 edition).

2. *Narrative of the Life of Frederick Douglass*, 118-119.

3. *Narrative of the Life of Frederick Douglass*, 121.

4. For more on this, see Francis Lyall, *Slaves, Citizens, Sons: Legal Metaphors in the Epistles* (Grand Rapids: Zondervan Publishing House, 1984).

3.

We Do Not Walk Alone

2 Timothy 1:1–2:26

Claim Your Story

Some years ago, the NBC network launched what became a hit series of telecasts with its program *Who Do You Think You Are?* The series featured several celebrity figures and the results of their quest to discover and explore their respective family tree. It was a show about genealogy, about tracing one's roots, one's family line, a subject that has become wildly popular. This interest in who we are, who our ancestors were, and where we came from, seems rooted in our psyche, which helps explain why the quest to know one's family history can be such a consuming passion.

What is bequeathed to us from previous generations, from our parents and others, influences us for good or ill. When that influence is strongly negative, even destructive, we may need the healing guidance of a psychotherapist. But our psychological and spiritual inheritance can also be positive and life-giving. When we recognize and claim that positive inheritance, we never really walk alone. Oprah Winfrey, an exceptionally creative businesswoman and one of the world's best-known television personalities, understands this. Mindful of those who went before her as family, and grateful for what their strivings helped her achieve, Ms. Winfrey has stated that whenever she has a big decision to make, she goes into her closet and sits and recites the names of her ancestors. Saying their names blesses her with caution, self-esteem, energy, and the inspiration to dare, knowing that she does not walk alone as she decides and acts.[1] Who is it who walks with you?

Enter the Bible Story

The importance of family in nurturing a healthy sense of self helps to explain the engagingly personal tone that we sense in the letter preserved in the New Testament canon as the second letter Paul the apostle wrote to Timothy, one of his closest associates. Paul writes as Timothy's "father" in the faith, as indeed he was. Paul addressed him here as "my dear child" (2 Timothy 1:2), using the same affectionate designation he used about Timothy in his letter to Corinth (1 Corinthians 4:17, "my loved and trusted child in the Lord").

Paul begins this letter to Timothy by paying tribute first to Paul's own forebears, and next to two of the young church leader's immediate forebears, his grandmother Lois and his mother Eunice (2 Timothy 1:3-5). Their lives and instruction had steadied Timothy in the Jewish tradition and readied him for the twice-born life of the Christian he had become through contact with Paul (see Acts 16:1-5).

Paul is in confinement as he writes, chained in a jail in Rome (2 Timothy 1:16-17; 2:9). His thoughts, however, are not on himself but on Timothy, his delegated emissary to Ephesus. Aware that Timothy was feeling the pressures of giving oversight to the church there, Paul was solicitous about Timothy's welfare and felt constrained to encourage him. Paul's charge to Timothy to "revive God's gift" that was in him (1:6) and the admonition that followed, that "God didn't give us a spirit that is timid but one that is powerful, loving, and self-controlled" (1:7), suggest that Timothy needed to exercise more "drive" and show more daring to manage his assignment effectively. The admonition allows us a limited look at Timothy's personality.

Was Timothy limited in his ministry by excessive modesty and shyness? Had Onesiphorus given Paul an assessment of Timothy's ministry in Ephesus as well as an update on church conditions in Ephesus during his trip from that city to visit the imprisoned apostle (1:16-18)? We have no way of knowing. But knowing Timothy, and knowing Ephesus, Paul sensed the need to share his heart anew with the young leader and the need to encourage him. Paul wrote this second letter to encourage and "fire him up" so that Timothy could effectively manage his assignment and the emotions that assignment inevitably stirred.

Paul had been the central figure in Timothy's training for ministry. After meeting him at Lystra (Acts 16:1-3), Paul had helped Timothy navigate the transition from being a novice to becoming Paul's able associate. Now, ministering on Paul's behalf at Ephesus, Timothy was probably feeling like he was on his own. Had he chafed, finding so much to work against (2 Timothy 2:16-18, 23; 3:1-9, 12-13; 4:3-5)? Or did he feel limited because too few were working with him? Was Timothy feeling hemmed in by aggressive false teachers? Was he discouraged that too little seemed under his control? Was he feeling increasingly limited and lonely without Paul's active presence? Whatever the conditions at Ephesus and within himself, Timothy was charged by Paul to remember the gifts of God in his life and stir himself to realize what those gifts mean and offer.

Entrusted With a Commission

Conversion, truly experienced, is designed to have a defining influence in shaping the believer's personality and behavior, but conversion is only the initial stage of a continuing process with which we must cooperate. That process is growth in grace, which is why Paul always greeted the churches to which he wrote, and the persons to whom he addressed letters, with a prayer that God and Christ grant "grace" and "peace" to them. Here in 2 Timothy 1:2, Paul's prayerful greeting includes a concern that "peace" be among the benefits accorded to Timothy.

Timothy needed to sense the peace of God as he sought to carry out his assignment. There were solemnly delegated duties to fulfill: There was the basic duty of giving "testimony about the Lord" (1:8). There was the duty to promote sound teaching (1:13), to protect that teaching (1:14), and to see that teaching passed on "to faithful people who are also capable of teaching others" (2:2). The Word was to be preached, erroneous teachings were to be corrected, false teachers confronted, and believers encouraged (4:2). These were solemn duties, and handling them would require self-discipline, courage to work, and an inward peace to govern inevitable feelings of honor or hurt as people received or rejected the one engaged in these duties.

"So, don't be ashamed," Paul advised. Christianity had not yet become "respectable," and some hearers would revile the message about Jesus as ignoble and view his death as dishonorable. Timothy would need to remember that salvation is based on that death, and he would need to rejoice that through dying Jesus "destroyed death and brought life and immortality into clear focus through the good news" (1:10b). It was precisely for testifying about that, Paul explained, that he himself was suffering; "but I'm not ashamed" (1:12).

Paul tells Timothy not to be ashamed of what was happening to him, his mentor, because the cause in which they both were engaged is "by God's will, to promote the promise of life that is in Christ Jesus" (1:1). Paul further explained that "God is the one who saved and called us with a holy calling" (1:9a) and that anyone's personal experience of salvation is a reason to feel honored, not ashamed. "This [salvation] wasn't based on what we have done, but it was based on his own purpose and grace that he gave us in Christ Jesus before time began" (1:9b).

Something happens through the gospel that humans cannot effect on their own; righteous living is granted by God's gracious deed in Christ, and this is cause to rejoice. Through the gospel—the testimony regarding Jesus—God calls humans into a new life, a holy, wholesome life. To accept salvation is to have a life so distinctive in behavior and so noble in character that there is nothing shameful about it. So, if one suffers for accepting God's call to that life, and for witnessing about the Jesus whose life and death made that call possible, then so be it. A life lived in accordance with the will of God inevitably sometimes places the believer in conflict with evil in the world. Thus Paul's bracing words to Timothy to "share the suffering for the good news, depending on God's power" (1:8b). Timothy can take comfort that God's power assists believers whenever they suffer for doing good.

Unlike some others in Ephesus who were ashamed when Paul was arrested for his preaching, Onesiphorus did not let the matter rest there; he stuck his neck out by continuing to support Paul (1:16). Onesiphorus knew Paul. He had worked with the apostle in establishing the gospel at Ephesus. So proud was Onesiphorus of Paul and his commitment to the Lord, he went to Rome after Paul was transferred there for trial so that he could be of service to him: "After I arrived in Rome, he quickly looked for me and found me" (1:17). He did so despite the social stigma attached to being a friend of a prisoner. By his visits, Onesiphorus actually opened himself to being labeled as a social deviant, a friend of a person publicly disgraced as a troublemaker and criminal, and even to be harshly treated by hard-nosed guards and unjust prison officials for just coming around. Some money-hungry official might have even sought to make him pay to gain access to Paul. No harassment or possible problems stopped Onesiphorus from visiting Paul in that Roman prison. Onesiphorus knew the blessing of being saved, and he treasured his friendship with the man whose message introduced him to the gospel. Those visit(s) encouraged Paul; they boosted his morale. Like Paul, Onesiphorus did not fear for himself; he was convinced that sharing in suffering never fails to gain its reward. Paul gratefully voiced a prayer for Onesiphorus and his entire household: "May the Lord show mercy to Onesiphorus' household, because he supported me many times [in Ephesus] and he wasn't ashamed of my imprisonment [in Rome]" (1:16).

Enduring With Integrity

Determined to motivate Timothy to be more fearless and to move forward, Paul instructed him to draw strength from the grace that is in Christ Jesus and "accept your share of suffering like a good soldier of Christ Jesus" (2:3). The military image was an apt one, with soldiers and guards always visible as key figures there in Paul's jail.

About the Scripture

Paul's Admiration for the Soldier Image

Soldiers were key figures throughout the Roman world. The Roman armies were responsible for security and keeping the peace, but they were also Rome's chief means in furthering Roman civilization. A trained soldier was more than an agent of security; a trained soldier reflected a culture. Soldiers supervised the building of roads, repaired aqueducts, and managed many public works across the Empire. Paul's admiration for the soldier image, however, might have been based on such other facts as these: that a trained soldier represents an ordered life, is loyal to an oath, can carry heavy loads, can manage strain, knows how to fight, and is always obedient to some "standard."[2] These were the features about which Paul was thinking when he referred to being "a good soldier of Christ Jesus."

Timothy is told to fan the flame of his courage into an even brighter fire by remembering those who had held a "standard" before him: Paul (1:11-13; 2:2), whom he knew at close range, but mainly Jesus, in whom he had placed his faith and gained new life. "Remember Jesus Christ, who was raised from the dead" (2:8). The emphasis was to keep on thinking about Jesus, so as to regard his own suffering as purposeful and to follow Jesus' example with unflagging zeal. Jesus' suffering did not last; it ended, and with a victorious result. The importance of sharing the good news about that result deserves full attention and unceasing action. "This is why I endure everything [even being imprisoned and chained here like a criminal] for the sake of those who are chosen by God so that they too may experience salvation in Christ Jesus with eternal glory" (2:10). Paul then rounded out his charge by quoting a poetic fragment from the church's "reliable sayings" tradition about the benefits every believer is promised if we meet Christ's faithfulness to us with faithfulness to him (2:11-12):

"If we have died together, we will also live together.
If we endure, we will also rule together.
If we deny him, he will also deny us."

But all is not lost if we sometimes falter. God expects spiritual progress, not spiritual perfection.

> "[Even] if we are disloyal, he stays faithful
> because he can't be anything else than what he is" (2:13).

Maintaining a God-Approved Status

There is no shame associated with the gospel, and Paul told Timothy there must be no shame associated with what happens to those who are faithful in handling it (1:8, 12, 16). Paul reminds Timothy about how to avoid the shame that matters, namely shame before God (2:14-26). Paul offers instruction about how to remain an approved worker in God's church.

1. Engage only in useful talk, in talk that profits others by building them up in the faith (2:14, 16-18). Uninformed and ill-informed disputes foment conflict and undermine community.
2. Zealously maintain the approval of God as a competent handler of the gospel, a worker who delivers the message of truth correctly (2:15). Only so can one deal aptly with ideas and teachings that "lead into ungodly behavior" (2:16) and undermine the spiritual health of the people (2:17). Competency requires disciplined diligence in living a true believer's life, in speaking the language of truth, and in labors that promote that truth.
3. Control your senses and the sensibilities that characterize your age group (2:22). How? By pursuing "righteousness, faith, love, and peace together with those who confess the Lord with a clean heart." A young leader is being told to be on guard against being victimized physically by strong sensual yearnings, on the one hand, and being carried along emotionally by the winds of novelty, on the other hand. The "run away from"/ "instead pursue" instruction told Timothy to concentrate on righteousness.

Our human experience includes some natural "cravings" (2:22), inclinations, and inborn passions that bid for our attention. These cravings can contribute to our well-being, and even renew us. They are best managed when resisted as controlling forces and are directed according to divine standards. Pursuing righteousness undergirds that kind of management, and we are helped with that management "through the Holy Spirit who lives in us" (1:14; see also 1:7). Our self-interest as Christians recognizes more than our physical senses and the sensibilities stimulated by much in popular culture. The Christian's self-interest is stimulated by divine truth that enlightens the conscience, guides the life in "righteousness, faith, love, and peace," and promotes togetherness with all who "confess the Lord with a clean heart" (2:22).

The apostle's mention in 2 Timothy 2:20-21 of choice vessels used in a mansion was meant to increase Timothy's sense of honor as one of the Lord's chosen servants. Knowing that the finest vessels owned would be displayed and used during festive occasions in the household, Timothy was to view his role in the church at Ephesus as one of honor, not shame, however menacing and demeaning the work and wiles of his opponents. "The Lord knows the people who belong to him," Paul declared, and Timothy was to take courage knowing that he was one among them. With his God-approved status, Timothy had no reason to be afraid or ashamed.

Live the Story

Paul's instructions to Timothy in this second letter appear to suggest that the young leader had run into circumstances that were like a wall in his path. The wall seemed high and thick, and he felt blocked from doing what he was sent to Ephesus to do.

Timothy also felt timid as he sought a way to move beyond the wall in his path. False teachings were part of that wall, and false teachers were a persistent and ever-present problem. His feelings were awry. He felt weary, inadequate, injured, ashamed, and awkward.

With what emotions are you wrestling as you seek to live out your Christian faith? What problems are you facing that test your mettle as a believer? What injuries have you sustained because of your service for the Lord?

This letter to Timothy helps us brace ourselves to accept suffering. It helps us know why the gospel is so offensive to some people, and why those associated with spreading the gospel are sometimes misunderstood, maligned, and mistreated. This letter also encourages us by its openness about sharing our feelings. Paul openly shared his feelings with Timothy, who was faltering as he dealt with his. Yes, problems happen as we live our faith and seek to share that faith with others. Yes, injuries sustained in our work hurt, and they drain us of energy. But while conflicts sometimes shake us, they can also shape us. Feeling vulnerable as a human is inevitable, but faith helps us accept that vulnerability as a valuable entry point for grace, knowing that we are not our own, we do not walk alone. "God is powerful enough to protect what he has placed in [our] trust until that day" (1:12).

Charles A. Tindley (1856?–1933) was mindful of this and was encouraged by this across a lifetime of ministry that included much stress and strain. But he was determined not to fail the Lord. Sincere in heart, he kept his life governed by standards and wrote a song that explains his stamina: he let "Nothing between [his] soul and the Savior."

> Nothing between, e'en many hard trials,
> though the whole world against me convene;
> watching with prayer and much self-denial,
> I'll triumph at last, there's nothing between.[3]

---

1. See Henry Louis Gates, Jr., *Finding Oprah's Roots: Finding Your Own* (New York: Crown Publishers, 2007).

2. For more on this, see G. R. Watson, *The Roman Soldier* (Ithaca, NY: Cornell University Press, 1969).

3. C. A. Tindley, "Nothing Between," *The United Methodist Hymnal* (Copyright © 1989 by The United Methodist Publishing House), 373.

4.

The Comfort and Counsel
That Sustain Us

2 Timothy 3:1–4:22

Claim Your Story

Every parent or guardian has had the sometimes difficult task of helping a child get through a painful experience of being harassed or hurt by someone else, perhaps a childhood bully, or worse, a selfish and insensitive adult. In addition to giving comfort, there is the need to let the child vent, discuss his or her attitude about what happened, seek to clarify his or her perception of why the happening took place, and discuss options on how to prevent it or handle it the next time around. Central to the parent's or guardian's concern, however, is how to help the child regain or retain his or her self-esteem after experiencing inward pain. It is no small thing to be criticized, slighted, ridiculed, bullied, verbally abused, or physically assaulted.

You will surely remember some occasion during your childhood when something hurtful happened to you. Hearing hurtful words directed against you, perhaps? Or being mocked because of your size or weight or appearance, or where you lived, how you dressed, or your gender, race, or ethnic heritage? You will remember that experiencing trouble in such ways, either for the first time or more than once, confused your mind and disabled your sense of self until some adult reached you in a timely fashion to provide comfort and clarifying counsel. So much of personal steadiness depends upon the comfort and counsel we receive from those who matter to us, especially our parents or guardians and our mentors.

Howard Thurman, one of the major religious leaders during the twentieth century, used to laud how his grandmother's presence and counsel blessed him and his sisters during their childhood years in their hometown of Daytona Beach, Florida. Nancy Ambrose was her name, and Thurman credited her with a special sensitivity about his inner need for validation as he grew up there in Daytona Beach where the "white and black worlds were separated by a wall of quiet hostility and overt suspicion." More than anyone else, he explained, she helped him sense his significance as a person and grow up with a healthy self-regard.

When Nancy Ambrose sensed that happenings in their lives might threaten to subdue them inwardly, she would gather Howard and his sisters and tell them a story based on her life as a former slave, a story that never failed to lift their spirits and strengthen their inner core. His grandmother would tell how she listened as a young girl to a certain slave preacher whose counsel helped her stand up to life. That preacher was allowed to address the slaves periodically, not regularly, but when he did, no matter the sermon subject, he always closed the sermon the same way and with the same words. After climaxing the sermon by dramatizing the crucifixion and resurrection of Jesus, he would pause, and with his eyes fixed scrutinizingly on each listener, he would tell them: "You are not niggers! You are not slaves! You are God's children!"[1] When the slave preacher had finished, the people's spirits were restored. And when Grandma Nancy had finished telling Howard and his sisters this, they were readied again to face life in segregated Daytona Beach.

Who helped you get ready for life's troubles? How timely was their help? How valid was that early counsel for the troubles you later met and for handling the transitions you have had to maneuver as you moved into the years? As you think about those who helped ready you for life's troubles and transitions, you will more readily appreciate the role the apostle Paul played in readying and steadying Timothy as a church leader and how Timothy would understandably trust and treasure the counsel preserved in the letters he received from his saintly mentor.

Enter the Bible Story

Near the beginning of this letter Paul expressed his desire to see Timothy (1:4), mindful of how the young man had wept when they parted. Timothy was one whose presence was a boon; his steady companionship in ministry was viewed as a gift from God, an expression to the older Paul of God's grace to him. Their like-mindedness was not based on a similar make-up but on spiritual bonding and a genuine concern for others. Paul had openly stated this to the believers at Philippi in Timothy's honor: "I have no one like him. He is a person who genuinely cares about your well-being" (Philippians 2:20).

Perilous Times Ahead

In 2 Timothy 3:1-9, Paul informs Timothy that more troublesome times are ahead and that evidences of this were already visible. "Understand that the last days will be dangerous times" (verse 1). Paul's list of dangers expected during "the last days" reads like a current news media account of urban life in our time, although it represents what Paul saw happening already in the Roman world before his eyes. Crimes and vices abounded then, and still abound, due to selfishness and the love of money (3:2a). As for our times, arrogance, bragging, and pride are daily reflected in events, articles, books, and newscasts, while slander is the expected order of the day as candidates for political offices jostle for position and power. Disobedience to parents is rife, along with ingratitude, the lack of holiness, the absence of affection, and a persistent stubbornness that resists cultivating peaceful relations. All these are characteristic evils in our time, as in Paul's (3:2b). So is the absence of self-control, a blatant will to be brutal, and an utter hatred of what is good (verse 3). Disloyalty, recklessness, and conceit

---

Across the Testaments

Pharaoh's Magicians

Second Timothy 3:8 mentions *Jannes* and *Jambres*, the names traditionally given to the magicians of Pharaoh's court who opposed Moses. While not mentioned in Exodus 7:11, 22, the names are found in the Targums (later Aramaic paraphrases of the Hebrew text) and in the Dead Sea Scrolls.

abound. The love of pleasure has eclipsed all other loves, even any love for God (verse 4). Even religious folk do not serve religion's proper end; they prioritize their own concerns but not the true concerns of God for true righteousness and human good. With evil on the rise, the church will suffer as people violently oppose the truth (verses 8-9).

Timothy is to continue following the example Paul set before him, paying strict "attention to [Paul's] teaching, conduct, purpose, faithfulness, patience, love, and endurance" (3:10). Timothy is reminded about having seen Paul handle many troubles, and a few of the places where those troubles were faced are mentioned: Antioch, Iconium, and Lystra— Timothy's hometown. The abuses were many, but "the Lord rescued me from it all!" Paul explained. Then he solemnly warned, "In fact, anyone who wants to live a holy life in Christ Jesus will be harassed" (3:12). As the evil-doing grows worse, and as deceived people deceive still others, Timothy must continue in the truth, remembering with regard those who taught him and living by the holy Hebrew Scriptures—those sacred writings which are "inspired by God and [are] useful for teaching, for showing mistakes, for correcting, and for training character, so that the person who belongs to God can be equipped to do everything that is good" (3:16-17).

Influenced more by his Jewish mother and grandmother than by his Greek father, Timothy had known the Hebrew Scriptures from his childhood. He was therefore aware of the voices and virtues and visions in the Scriptures; those voices recounted experiences with God, and those virtues and visions had illumined his mind and challenged his life. Those Scriptures foreshadowed and foretold the coming and work of the Christ about whom Paul preached, and for whom Paul lived. Through those Scriptures Timothy had become "wise in [the] way that leads to salvation through faith that is in Christ Jesus" (3:15). Despite the crimes, chaos, and confusion in society, Timothy is told that staying with the Scriptures, and living by the wisdom deposited there, would help him to stay "equipped to do everything that is good" (verse 17).

Timothy is therefore charged anew—as if in a courtroom where God and Christ Jesus are present as witnesses to this solemn event—to "preach the word" (the message of salvation), mindful of its importance to himself and all others at the coming return of Christ Jesus "to judge the living and the dead," at the time of "his appearance and his kingdom" (4:1-2). As a servant of that word, Timothy must be a man for all seasons. He must be ready to preach that word "whether it is convenient or inconvenient," using it to "correct, confront, and encourage with patience and instruction" (4:2). Some people will not applaud his work, he was told, they will oppose it, eager rather to listen to others whose message will please and promote their self-interests. Some will yearn for myths, not the gospel (4:4), eager to explore stories, practices, and happenings that stimulate the imagination rather than deal with biblical verities and values that produce godliness. Timothy is told to stay focused, disciplined, and accepting of any suffering associated with carrying out his service (4:5).

Paul Anticipates His Final Transition

Paul was no stranger to transitions; he had weathered many changes across his life. In fact, his life was filled with transition experiences, and he used the wisdom gained from those experiences to instruct and encourage the churches he founded and served. Paul openly shared his secret of coping well with troubles and transitions when—writing from a jail cell—he told the Philippians: "I have learned how to be content in any circumstance. I know the experience of being in need and of having more than enough; I have learned the secret to being content in any and every circumstance, whether full or hungry or whether having plenty or being poor. I can endure all these things through the power of the one who gives me strength" (Philippians 4:11-13). Every trouble and transition Paul experienced renewed him for his work. He did not deny the impact he felt when troubles blocked his path; he admitted that they hurt and sometimes confused him: "We are experiencing all kinds of trouble," he told the Corinthians, "but we aren't crushed. We are confused, but we aren't depressed. We are harassed, but we aren't abandoned. We are knocked down, but we aren't knocked out" (2 Corinthians 4:8-9). Paul knew that he could not control his circumstances, but he was confident that God was in control of how those circumstances would be used for good (Romans 8:28).

Here, now, was another transition point in Paul's life: his transition from this life to the next, through death. Timothy needed to know and respond to what Paul was sensing, and he needed to know it and respond in time to visit the apostle before the end came. Thus Paul's request: "Do your best to come to me quickly" (2 Timothy 4:9).

Endings are events that we dread. Making a farewell speech, or hearing someone make one, stirs deep emotions. Paul's feelings are on display when he writes, "I'm already being poured out like a sacrifice to God, and the time of my death is near" (4:6). The confession is taut and telling, strikingly open in its tone of resignation. He makes a brief reference to his struggles, his pursuit, and his persistence: "I have fought the good fight, finished the race, and kept the faith" (4:7), and his use of the perfect tense evidences his sense that his ministry is facing its end.

Paul does not view death's approach as a sad ending, but rather a transition point for a new beginning. He had preached the life *of* Christ and had experienced life *in* Christ; soon, he sensed, he would enjoy life *with* Christ, the righteous Judge, and be crowned by him with "the champion's wreath that is awarded for righteousness" (4:8). Clearly, facing death did not diminish Paul's expectation of good. Like the psalmist, Paul was convinced that goodness and mercy were guarding him, and that he would "dwell in the house of the LORD forever" (Psalm 23:6, NIV). Paul's anticipation that his death was near is more than one of resignation, it is a statement as well of expected good. For believers, death does not mean the final end, it means fulfillment. And the champion's wreath belongs not only to faithful apostles of the Lord "but also to all those who have set their heart on waiting for his appearance" (2 Timothy 4:8b).

Shared News About the Pauline Circle

Having reported where some of the others within his ministry circle were, and what they were doing (4:10-15), Paul tells Timothy what took place during his initial trial, how things went: "No one took my side at my first court hearing. Everyone deserted me" (4:16). Had Paul gone to that hearing expecting legal assistance that was not provided? Had he expected certain believers to speak on his behalf, and they failed to show? Whatever the circumstantial details of the disappointment Paul experienced, he here forgives and prays for those who disappointed him. Lacking legal or other assistance when the charges listed against him were read and heard, Paul solemnly spoke in his own defense. Blessed by the Lord, Paul's witness was substantial, strong, significant, and apparently sufficient, because he was "rescued from the lion's mouth!" (4:17).

The mention of a "first court hearing" implies that there was a later, "second" hearing. Since Paul testifies here of having been "rescued from the lion's mouth," the reader might conclude that in mentioning the first court hearing he was thinking back on the release he had gained from his earlier imprisonment in Rome (see Acts 28:30). During that imprisonment, "Paul was permitted to live by himself, with a soldier guarding him" (28:16). That confinement allowed Paul certain privileges: he "lived in his own rented quarters for two full years and welcomed everyone who came to see him. Unhindered and with complete confidence, he continued to preach God's kingdom and to teach about the Lord Jesus Christ" (28:30-31).

This second letter to Timothy reflects a later period in Paul's life, and a second imprisonment in Rome. This time there are no privileges: Paul is being treated "like a common criminal" (2 Timothy 2:9); and this time he senses that death will be his deliverer. Thus his bold claim: "The Lord will rescue me from every evil action and will save me for his heavenly kingdom. To him be the glory forever and always. Amen" (4:18). For Paul, death would rescue him from any more trouble and any further transitions.

The letter closes with greetings to Prisca and Aquila, a wife and husband who were fellow tentmakers like Paul and longtime associates with him in church planting (Acts 18:1-4, 18-21; 1 Corinthians 16:19); they were back in Ephesus after a time in Rome (Romans 16:3-4). Members of the household of Onesiphorus are also greeted. This second mention in this letter of that leader and his household (2 Timothy 1:16-18; 4:19) not only shows Paul's regard for Onesiphorus—who is never directly addressed—but also Paul's appreciation for the household's acceptance of

Onesiphorus's absence during the visit he made to Paul in Rome. Perhaps the lack of a direct greeting is because this friend had recently died. If so, then the feeling associated with that loss, and the remembered illness of Trophimus, stirred Paul to repeat his plea for Timothy to come to Rome and see him. He had already written, "Do your best to come to me quickly" (4:9), bringing Mark and some chosen books (verses 11, 13). Now he urgently asks Timothy to "try hard to come to me before winter" (4:21a), to arrive before November, when regular ship travel on the Mediterranean Sea would close down until the spring. Paul sensed that he might not live that long.

Did Timothy get to Rome before Paul died? We ask, but cannot know, all accounts from reputed "tradition" notwithstanding. What we do know is that Paul the apostle, Timothy's mentor, died in Rome, a martyr for Jesus Christ the Lord, in A.D. 67 or 68. We also know from the Letter to the Hebrews that Timothy, Paul's "beloved son in the faith" and chief emissary, underwent imprisonment at some point later than Paul's second letter to him, and that he was in time set free (Hebrews 13:23). Paul's counsel to this "son in the faith" was not only direct, needed, and timely, it was also Spirit-directed. Let us rejoice that this letter has been preserved for us within the canon of Christian Scriptures. The church has recognized that this letter, like the Hebrew Scriptures it lauds, was "inspired by God and is useful for teaching, for showing mistakes, for correcting, and for training character, so that the person who belongs to God can be equipped to do everything that is good" (2 Timothy 3:16-17).

Live the Story

We too are in transition. Life has us moving on, and the stages we meet during our journey forward will test us in both expected and unexpected ways. We are all heirs of emotional distress, anxious states of mind, health disorders, and sometimes a troubled soul. Fears can alarm us, troubles depress us, and circumstances confuse us. We can feel imprisoned in more than a physical way. Paul's open secret about coping remains, and it can guide us to a full-orbed faith in the One who saved us: "I'm convinced that God is powerful enough to protect what he has placed in my trust until that day" (2 Timothy 1:12b). Such a faith can sustain us whatever the shape or size of our troubles and the dizzying number of transitions we experience.

Faith is strengthened as we "remember Jesus Christ, who was raised from the dead" (2:8). Faith is also strengthened through the counsel and comfort of the Scriptures. Like Paul and Timothy, we must *know* the Scriptures, we must trust their wisdom, and we must follow their guidance to discover our mistakes, correct our errors, and receive character training in righteousness.

Like Paul and Timothy, we should take time to recall the persons who helped us get ready for life, those whose presence and counsel helped us to get through troubles and cope with our transitions. Call out their names in grateful thanks to God, and if some of them are yet alive, pray for them and follow that prayer with a call or letter to them if they live at a distance. The deepest thanks, though, will reveal itself when we emulate the care they showed by caring for others in their need. We prove ourselves grateful when we pass on to others what was passed on to us.

As in Paul's life, God's concerns must be our concerns, and those concerns must remain our priority, with our hearts willing to accept any suffering associated with living as we should and laboring where we are sent. As Charles Wesley writes in his well-known hymn,

> A charge to keep I have,
> a God to glorify,
> a never-dying soul to save,
> and fit it for the sky.
>
> To serve the present age,
> my calling to fulfill;
> O may it all my powers engage
> to do my Master's will![2]

---

1. *With Head and Heart: The Autobiography of Howard Thurman* (New York: Harcourt Brace Jovanovich, 1979), 10, 20-21.

2. Charles Wesley, "A Charge to Keep I Have," stanzas 1 and 2, in *The United Methodist Hymnal* (Copyright © 1989 by The United Methodist Publishing House), 413.

5.

Living Faithfully in a Hostile Environment

Paul's Letter to Titus

Claim Your Story

Several years ago, Academy Award-winning actor Denzel Washington starred in the popular movie *Remember the Titans.* Inspired by real events, the film is set in 1971 Alexandria, Virginia, at the recently desegregated T. C. Williams High School. Washington plays African American Herman Boone, who has been hired as the new head coach of the football team. Early on, Boone encounters a threatened boycott by the white players on the team. He faces sustained hostility from school board members and others in the community. Boone, working with white assistant coach (and former head coach) Bill Yoast, leads the Titans to stunning success on the gridiron. But even more impressive than the Titans' undefeated season is Boone's confident, uncompromising leadership in a hostile environment.

When have you found yourself in an uncomfortable and hostile environment? Maybe it happened at school or in the neighborhood. Perhaps it happened on the job, in the factory, office, or shop. Maybe it happened in a church. Was the hostility due to the color of your skin? To your ethnic heritage? To your financial status? Perhaps the hostility was occasioned by a clash of values, a situation in which others covertly or overtly pressured you to do something that you felt was wrong.

The conflict of values and the scope of hostility can be very local or they can extend across an entire society. In any case, followers of Jesus face a challenge. How can we maintain our integrity in a hostile environment? How can we live godly lives in a sometimes ungodly environment? How can we resist the proclivity to sinfulness that we encounter in situations that surround us on a daily basis—and if we are honest, that we encounter within our own selves? These are the issues that preoccupy the apostle Paul in his Letter to Titus.

Enter the Bible Story

The Letter to Titus opens with a dense greeting as Paul links the leading themes of the gospel message with the divine background of his authority to proclaim that message. After giving his name and two designations for himself—"a slave of God" and "an apostle of Jesus Christ"—Paul then declares his assigned work: "to bring about the faith . . . and a knowledge of the truth that agrees with godliness" (Titus 1:1). The basis for this "faith" and "knowledge" is God's promise to grant eternal life to all who believe on God, a promise that was voiced by the prophets, publicized in the Scriptures, and now continues to be extended through preaching (1:2). That, Paul proudly asserts, is his work, and he confesses that he "was trusted with preaching this message by the command of God our savior" (1:3). Paul will say more about "faith," "a knowledge of the truth," "godliness," "hope," and "eternal life" in this letter.

The greeting is addressed to "Titus, my true child in a common faith" (1:4).

Concerning Titus the Man

Titus, like Timothy, was one of Paul's converts. Thus that tender expression of closeness, "my true child in a common faith." Like Timothy, Titus was an associate Paul trusted with handling strategic ministry assignments. We know less about Titus than about Timothy, but we know that he was a prized associate within Paul's ministry circle.

Among the known facts regarding Titus are these: He was a Gentile, the son of Greek parents, and he was probably from Antioch. Based on details supplied in Paul's second letter to the church at Corinth, Titus was Paul's primary messenger and delegate to that church when Paul, the founding leader, had to be absent from them (2 Corinthians 7:7, 13-14).

Titus was the one Paul entrusted with organizing the collection of relief funds sent from the Corinthians and other churches of Macedonia to the needy Jewish believers in Jerusalem (8:16-24).

Titus's Pastoral Task on Crete

The Letter to Titus locates him in Crete, a Greek island located southeast of the mainland and at the southern limit of the Aegean Sea. Titus is in Crete at Paul's directive to accomplish two main tasks within and for the churches there: first, "to organize whatever needs to be done," and second, "to appoint elders in each city" (1:5).

When Paul ministered on Crete is not clear. The reports given in the Acts of the Apostles about Paul's travels do not mention him going to Crete, but since in Romans 15:19 Paul mentioned having preached "from Jerusalem all the way around to Illyricum," and since he added that he did not "have any place to work in [those] regions anymore" (Romans 15:23), it is possible that Paul had some contact with people on (or from?) Crete during his voyage to Rome (see Acts 27–28), or perhaps after his release from his first imprisonment in Rome. Although we have no written record about any visit by Paul to Crete, Paul states in the Letter to Titus that he "left" Titus behind there to manage some matters left unsettled or unfinished earlier. Those matters included appointing and installing "elders" and "overseers" for the church(es) there.

The Elder/Overseer Qualities

The status and services of "elders" and/or "overseers" oblige them to be (and remain) unimpeachable in character (Titus 1:6a). This virtue is expected in the life of every believer, but it is highlighted here as a prerequisite for someone being appointed to lead or serve in a conspicuous spiritual role. If married, they should be known for faithfulness to their spouse. If they have children, the children should evidence lives of obedience and unselfishness (1:6b). The necessity that an elder's children be well-behaved is to point out that someone's management skills are best illustrated by positive effects in their own household, their own family setting. No family leader who is "stubborn, irritable, addicted to alcohol, a bully, or greedy" (1:7) would qualify for appointment, lacking both the personal virtues and the positive example necessary to influence the family for good. What is needed, and required, Paul states, are elders and overseers for each city who "show hospitality, love what is good, and [are] reasonable, ethical, godly, and self-controlled" (1:8). Each leader must evidence a well-ordered life: a life that evidences strict "attention to the reliable message as it has been taught to them so that they can encourage people with healthy instruction and refute those who speak against it" (1:9).

The Problematic Character of the Environment in Crete

Churches do not exist in a vacuum; their members are part and parcel of some larger populace. The Christian faith is personally received, but it is lived out in a societal setting. Paul wants the church members in Crete to understand the threats in their environment. One most immediate problem in the social environment of Crete was *religious opposition from Jews*. Paul primarily had in mind here not Jews as such but those within the church who taught that Gentile males must not only believe on Jesus but also be circumcised (submit to the Mosaic law) to be saved. Paul labels them "rebellious people, loudmouths" (1:10) and warns Titus that "they must be silenced because they upset entire households" (1:11).

Paul and Titus had clashed often with Christian Jews who insisted on making male Gentile believers observe the Jewish rite of circumcision. Paul had earlier solved the problem that this Jewish view posed in evangelizing Gentiles. In visiting any town or city, it was his practice to go first to the Jewish synagogue to share the gospel and only afterward to some convenient spot where he could address anyone who came; his reasoning was, as stated in Romans 1:16, "to the Jew first and also to the Greek." The problem surfaced when male Gentile converts and Christian Jews were members of the same assembly and were divided over the issue of what was required to be fully accepted by God. Acts 15:1-35 sheds light on how the apostles, elders, and Paul met early on during a called meeting in Jerusalem to settle the issue. The settlement ruled out requiring male Gentile believers to be circumcised. Titus, a Greek, was present with Paul at that meeting; as a result of that decision, he did not have to be circumcised (see Galatians 2:3).

The Godly Life and Its Basis in Grace

The "faith" and "knowledge of the truth" that Paul was commissioned by God to share through preaching have the goal of producing "godliness" (Titus 1:1), attitudes and behavior that reflect the character of God. Intent to show how godliness is evidenced in the believer's life, Paul briefly states how each believer is expected to relate within the closest spheres of contact: the home and household setting (2:1-10).

All talk should be "consistent with sound teaching" (2:1). Older adults are to live with dignity, be sensible about living, be healthy in their relationships, teach what is good, mentor the young adults about family togetherness, and exhibit an orderly home life. Paul knew that the strongest antidote to fight poison in an environment is a healthy home life.

The Letter to Titus doesn't explicitly challenge the conventional order within households in the Hellenistic world. Slaves in the household who are Christians should respect the over/under relationship, discipline their tongues, and never steal. "Instead they should show that they are completely reliable in everything so that they might make the teaching about God our savior attractive in every way" (2:10).

Paul, and everyone else in the Roman Empire, was familiar with the ancient and Empire-wide practice of owning and utilizing slaves. Paul did not attack that system frontally; he knew that challenging that system directly could jeopardize the church's freedom to exist openly and could have fatal consequences for him personally. Although Paul did not openly decry the slavery system, he systematically worked to undermine it in several ways. For instance, Paul openly opposed the slave trade, calling it "kidnapping" (1 Timothy 1:10), because slave trading violated the seventh commandment: "You shall not steal" (Exodus 20:15, NRSV). Further, when addressing Christian slaves in another setting, he advised, "[I]f you are actually able to be free, take advantage of the opportunity" (1 Corinthians 7:21b). Yet again, he encouraged Philemon, a slave owner who was a believer, to free Onesimus, one of his slaves who was converted after making contact with Paul (Philemon 15, 20-21). Admittedly, these occasional tactics amount to limited actions against the slavery system, but they were indications of Paul's own aversion to it.

As we will see below, Paul's chief concern is to proclaim the good news of God's gracious action in Christ. Nothing should be allowed to discredit that good news or to discourage its acceptance. Paul wants believers to behave in their household life in ways that draw the approval and respect of outsiders. Christians should ordinarily abide by community standards "so that God's word won't be ridiculed" and "so that any opponent will be ashamed because they won't find anything bad to say about us" (Titus 2:5, 8). By "us," Paul means the Christians.

Paul told Titus to "talk about these things. Encourage and correct with complete authority," and do not let anyone disrespect or disregard him (2:15). Titus had been given authority to speak the truth and apply that truth. Any teachings contrary to the knowledge of that truth were to be countered and corrected. The believers living in Crete needed to understand what constitutes a truly Christian life, and then to live it.

Managing close relations with a spouse and children without being selfish, and responding as a slave to unjust circumstances without rancor, requires something special within the heart and mind. It requires what Howard Thurman referred to as a "strength beyond our strength, giving strength to our strength."[1] So Paul went on to state in Titus 2:11 what that special something is: "the grace of God." He also spells out what that special something does: "The grace of God has appeared, bringing salvation to all people. It educates us so that we can live sensible, ethical, and godly lives right now by rejecting ungodly lives and the desires of this world" (2:11-12).

Paul preached and wrote a lot about the grace of God! More than ninety times he used the word *grace* in his letters. It is a common term throughout the New Testament because it is part of the vocabulary of the church. The apostle John, writing about Jesus, spoke of him as "full of grace and truth" (John 1:14). Here at Titus 2:11, Paul names God as the source of that grace, because it was God who sent Jesus to display his favor and kindness by saving people: "the grace of God has appeared."

The word *grace* (Greek: *charis*) was originally used to refer to the affective qualities of someone or something that pleased or delighted the beholding person. The word later expanded in meaning to include those affective qualities excited in the beholder. Still later, the New Testament writers used the term *grace* to mean the favor God extended to humans by meeting the human need to be forgiven and restored after having sinned.

Biblically understood, then, "the grace of God" is that accepting attitude on God's part that is expressed in granting humans mercy, forgiveness of sins, deliverance from the power of sin, and full adoption into the household of faith, and in granting us access to all the benefits associated with belonging to God's family. The acceptance of grace grants "salvation," and growing in that grace (2 Peter 3:17-18) is the process by which the believer develops in godliness. That growth enables the believer to combat the negatives from a problematic psychophysiological make-up, an unwholesome upbringing, a poisonous social environment, and the personal effects of sinful actions. This is the message of Titus 2:11-14. Accepting the grace of God rescues one from sin, educates one in righteousness, and motivates one to godly behavior and good actions. Such is the work of grace, that action of God in one's life that is efficient, sufficient, and abundant. The songwriter expressed it well: "Marvelous, infinite, matchless grace, freely bestowed on all who believe."[2]

About the Christian Faith

Justifying and Sanctifying Grace

The concept of grace permeates the Scriptures and the history of Christian teachings. The church has consistently affirmed the reality and importance of both *justifying grace* and *sanctifying grace*. While different church traditions may emphasize particular nuances of meaning, the central idea of *justifying grace* is that God has taken the initiative through Jesus Christ to save us from sin and guilt. Sin is so pervasive and so powerful that we cannot free ourselves. God rescues us from the bondage or controlling influence of sin. By God's gracious love, we are justified, that is, restored to a right relationship, a positive relationship, with God. Justification is not something we accomplish by willpower and effort; rather, it comes as a gift from a generous God.

Justification begins a changed condition in our lives. Our old nature begins to wane and a new creation emerges. God's *sanctifying grace* is at work in our lives so that we are, over time, more and more able to live as God intends us to live. Holy living is not an achievement; it's the result of the active work of the Holy Spirit in our lives. In sanctification, God again is first in action and we respond to and cooperate with that divine action.

The gospel message, fully accepted, can effect a change of consciousness. However marred by sin and destructive habits, we can undergo change in the way we perceive and behave. The salvation brought by God's grace introduces the believer to a new culture and a new way of responding to any and every environment. The salvation wrought in us by God's grace does not call for a retreat from life in the world; rather, it helps us to resist—and overcome—the ungodliness that is in the world. We who believe must live *in* the world, but we do not have to live *like* the world (see John 17:16). Whereas "we were once foolish, disobedient, deceived, and slaves to our desires and various pleasures too, . . . spending our lives in evil behavior and jealousy. We were disgusting" (Titus 3:3). But "when God our savior's kindness and love appeared, he saved us because of his mercy. . ." (3:4). "So, since we have been made righteous by his grace, we can inherit the hope for eternal life" (3:7). When Paul added, "This saying is reliable" (3:8), he was saying: You can count on being and receiving what God promised!

Among Paul's final instructions were these: He urged respect for rulers and civil authorities responsible for societal order (3:1). And he laid out a process for dealing with persons who cause conflict in the church (3:10-11). Any factious person should be admonished no more than twice, and if there is no change in their divisive behavior, then the person should be dismissed, knowing that he or she "is twisted and sinful" and does not belong in the fellowship. "Have nothing more to do with [that] person" (3:10). This judgment strikes modern ears as harsh. It's important to grasp the underlying logic here: by their persistent promotion of untruths, factions, and outright divisions, such persons have judged themselves.

Live the Story

Titus was left in Crete for a reason, for *a cause*. There was a purposefulness to his life that motivated him. That purpose enabled him to stay and work even in a place like Crete. You and I have been left where we are for a reason.

Titus's reason for being in Crete was not *casual*, he was not there by chance; his reason for being there was *causal*—the cause of the gospel, the cause his life served both in sound words and good deeds. Such is the mission of every Christian, and that mission proceeds best when we lead a godly life, sustained by a sense of the grace of God and a sensed place in his purpose—wherever we live. Fanny Crosby understood this, and wisely prayed:

> Consecrate me now to thy service, Lord,
>   by the power of grace divine;
>   let my soul look up with a steadfast hope,
>   and my will be lost in thine.[3]

1. Howard Thurman, *Meditations of the Heart* (New York: Harper and Brothers, 1953), page 95.
2. Julia H. Johnston, "Grace Greater than Our Sin," *The United Methodist Hymnal*, 365.
3. Fanny J. Crosby, "I Am Thine, O Lord," *The United Methodist Hymnal*, 419.

6.

Using Influence Unselfishly

Paul's Letter to Philemon

Claim Your Story

Think for a moment about the social layers in your community. Who is on top? Why are they there? Who is on the bottom? Why are they there? Where are you? What are the ramifications of one's position on the social ladder or social pyramid? Most of us have known persons who were granted deference because of their social standing. Some of us have seen or even been in situations when that preference denied fairness or justice to someone who lacked that standing.

So much of life in our urban, commercial, industrial, democratic society reflects social stratification that we tend to take it for granted as just part and parcel of our society. We are so accustomed to the all-too-common distinctions of rich/poor, or lower class/middle class/upper class, that we are apt to view this as normal, overlooking or forgetting that where someone is located within such distinctions often determines how she or he is understood, regarded, and valued.

In the place and time-period reflected in Paul's Letter to Philemon, social stratification included not only rich/poor, but *master/slave*; and reading this letter requires us to revisit what it can mean to someone low in the social system to be seen, understood, and treated as a person. Reading this letter also allows us to appreciate how Paul uses his standing and influence to change the state and status of someone who deserved that change.

Enter the Bible Story

Paul's Letter to Philemon is short, charmingly expressive, commendatory of Philemon, subtle in the request it makes to him, and loaded with social implications that are far-reaching. This brief letter—only 335 words in Greek—is one of the apostle's most private writings, although it deals with a matter of open social consequence, namely, the requested freeing of Onesimus, a slave belonging to Philemon. That this letter has been preserved as part of the New Testament is due perhaps to two factors: one, its message about what being fellow-members of the body of Christ means and demands, and two, the important ministry of the person on whose behalf the letter was composed and sent.

Philemon appears to have been a landowner, perhaps a businessman, a person of some wealth. His ordered life included a household that contained slaves. Philemon was a Christian believer, a man of generosity who used his house to host the believers who lived in and near Colossae, the city of his residence.

Address and Greetings

Paul addressed Philemon as "dearly loved coworker" (verse 1) and "partner" (verse 17), perhaps because he had worked with Paul in developing the church there, or because Philemon was steadily involved in ministry to the Christian group in Colossae and the surrounding territory. Being addressed as "coworker" might also indicate that Philemon was the principal leader of the group that met in his house.

Although Philemon is directly addressed, Paul also greets Apphia, Archippus, and "the church that meets in your house" (verse 2). The letter primarily involves Philemon, as the singular use of "you" and "your" clearly indicates (verses 4-21, 23). But the plural "you" in verses 3 and 25 suggests it was important to greet the other believers within the household because the import of the letter would impact not only Philemon but also the entire fellowship.

Paul's Recognition of Philemon

Paul encourages Philemon as an esteemed person on his prayer list. He extols Philemon's faithfulness and steady activities as a Christian and states that his prayer to God for Philemon was that the faith they shared in common ("your partnership in the faith," verse 6) would continue to be effective, enriched by increased understanding of what is good and what promotes the Christian faith. Paul then confesses and rejoices that Philemon's characteristic love and actions on behalf of believers in and around Colossae have given him joy and encouragement (verse 7). Perhaps Paul was not only thanking Philemon for using his position, skills, and resources to assist other believers, but encouraging him to continue doing so.

Paul's Request of Philemon

Given Philemon's characteristic openness and regard for persons in a plight, and particularly for those who are fellow-believers, Paul makes an appeal on behalf of someone who is both in a plight and a fellow-believer: Philemon's slave Onesimus. Paul speaks of Onesimus as "my child" (verse 10), having led him to Christ. Skillfully playing with words, Paul explains that while Onesimus might have previously been "useless" to Philemon, he was now "useful" to them both—that is, he was now in a position through Christ, his new Lord, to live up to his name (since the Greek *Onesimos* means "useful" or "profitable").

Why was Onesimus a slave? Had he been sold into slavery as a child? Had he been abandoned as an illegitimate child and retrieved from some village dump heap and reared in servitude? Was he the son of a slave mother? Did he sell himself into slavery to settle some debt? Had he been promised manumission (freedom) as reward for good work, but fallen into disfavor with his master, Philemon? Had he fulfilled the terms of his enslavement but was still in bondage because he was considered too valuable to lose? There is much about Onesimus that we do not know but wish we did.

There is still another question: What had Onesimus done, or not done, to be labeled "useless"? The term was commonly used in referring to a bad slave. Had he failed in some highly important assigned task? Had he run away to escape censure, or a worse punishment? If Onesimus had failed his master's trust in some way, and had fled the scene, he was not only a runaway, he was classified as a fugitive and was legally liable under Roman law.

About the Scripture

Slavery in the Hellenistic World

Slavery, which allowed one person to own another person, was a social institution almost universally accepted in the first-century Mediterranean world. Questions about the legitimacy of slavery were seldom raised; it was assumed to be a given and necessary part of the economic and social order.

Unlike the European and American slave trade, slavery in the Roman Empire was not race-based. Slaves could not be recognized on the street as slaves. One could become a slave because of any one of several factors: being born to slave parents, being abandoned as a baby, being kidnapped and sold, being a prisoner of war, or selling oneself into slavery to pay debts.

Regarded as property, slaves were vulnerable to extreme abuse. But many slaves were educated and served in important managerial roles. Slaves could be bought out of slavery by others, or if they were paid wages and could accumulate enough money were sometimes allowed to purchase their own freedom.

The New Testament provides ample evidence that Paul was not an avid supporter of slavery. More than that, the evidence suggests that Paul saw clearly the incongruity between slavery and Christian freedom, equality, and community. But Paul astutely recognized that assuming the role of an outspoken abolitionist would have put not only him but the entire fledgling Christian movement in jeopardy.

At some point during his departure, Onesimus made contact with Paul, who was in prison at the time. Where? We do not know for sure, since 2 Corinthians 11:23 mentions that Paul was imprisoned many times; but quite possibly the contact with Paul was made during his first imprisonment in Rome. Since Paul was incarcerated, the fact that Onesimus visited him in a prison seems more intentional than accidental. A legally liable fugitive would have sought to remain "on the run" rather than risk being captured. Whatever explains the encounter, Onesimus might well have remembered Paul from contact with him during Paul's ministry in Colossae and as a guest in Philemon's house. It is possible that Onesimus sought out Paul and visited him to gain his help to arbitrate some difference between Philemon (his master) and himself. What is clear in Paul's Letter to Philemon is that Onesimus was now converted and was returning to face his master. The letter implies some past wrong on his part, some wrong he was willing to answer for and make right, because he was now a Christian. Paul encouraged Onesimus to return to Philemon—thus to meet a legal demand—and Paul was requesting Philemon to receive Onesimus back, not as one to be punished but pardoned—thus to meet a Christian obligation to be reconciled. Paul was urging Philemon to lay aside any hard feelings and any sense of legal privilege and receive Onesimus back, forgiven; and he wanted Philemon to view Onesimus no longer as a slave to be controlled but as a brother to be encouraged and embraced.

But there was more to Paul's request: because Onesimus was now "a brother" (verse 16), he should not only be received in the spirit of recon-ciliation but should also be manumitted, released from his slave status, set free to be in service to Christ. It was in Philemon's power to do this, and Paul both urged and expected him to do it. Philemon owned Onesimus, and under Roman law he had the legal power to manumit him from his status as a slave. Paul expected Philemon to do just that. "Yes, brother, I want this favor from you in the Lord! Refresh my heart in Christ. I'm writ-ing to you, confident of your obedience and knowing that you will do more than what I ask" (verses 20-21).

Reviewing the Whole Issue

Paul's Letter to Philemon about Onesimus is actually a Christian response to the problem of socially sanctioned human slavery. Slavery was part and parcel of the social reality in the Greco-Roman world. The master/slave arrangement was so ingrained in the social order of that time that any opposition to it was viewed as being against the order of the Empire itself. As an apostle, a primary church leader in the first century, Paul had to address relations between persons in different social stations in society, some of them fixed differences that were acknowledged as legal and bind-ing. As part of the accepted order in life, those settings and stations could not be regarded as insignificant if the church wished to exist without being labeled as subversive. Much has been written about Paul's alleged acqui-escence with slavery, and his supposed allegiance and sense of privilege as a Roman citizen, but the letter he wrote to Philemon helps correct the picture that often appears in the literature about Paul.

Paul's Letter to Philemon is his attempt to deal in a Christian manner with the legal, moral, and social aspects of a broken relationship between a master and a slave, both of whom were Christians. The letter sheds light on class differences, human bondage, and legal demands. As for class differences, Paul asserted and affirmed his relationship to both Philemon and Onesimus, refusing to honor or prefer the master more than the slave. Both were persons of worth to Paul, and both were advised about how to deal with their broken relationship.

There was within Paul a strong sense of will to help persons. As he declared in 1 Corinthians 9:22, "I have become all things to all people, so I could save some by all possible means." Here, in this letter, we see Paul having become slave-minded, so as to understand Onesimus more fully, and using his influence with Philemon to facilitate their reconciliation— but with a wider scene in his view, namely that slave's freedom and possible fuller life as a coworker with him in the gospel. Working within the parameters of the law, he sought to move both Philemon and Onesimus beyond that law, influenced by Christian love.

Paul knew that slavery is not a good in itself, that it undermines human dignity and denies and distorts meaningful human relationships. Slavery has always been a system of bondage and control based on utility. The system subjects human beings to the will of others with the aim of economic gain for the persons who are in control. Any concern for the personal good of the slave is inextricably linked to continuing, enhancing, and guaranteeing that slave's availability and readiness to be used. Slaves are valued to the extent of their usefulness, and they are considered "good" mainly with reference to their handling of some ordered activity, not their character. Paul knew all of this. In fact, his training had acquainted him with the stipulation in the Torah against returning to some master a slave who managed to escape and find refuge in someone's custody (Deuteronomy 23:15). Roman law differed, with its demand that the runaway slave must be returned to the owner and that the one who harbors the fugitive is liable; so it was with the Fugitive Slave Acts passed by the

United States Congress centuries later to protect the interests and economies of America's slave-holding states. When Paul encouraged Onesimus to return to Philemon, it was not because he was honoring slavery as a good system, nor was he thinking only about what Roman law allowed and protected; rather, in sending Onesimus back to Philemon, Paul sought to use that law to go beyond it as an instance to teach believers about the meaning of grace and Christian fellowship. He wanted Philemon and Onesimus to move beyond the master/slave sense of over/under relation and experience each other in a higher frame of reference as brothers in Christ.

The injustice of being in bondage to another person, and being treated as mere property, stirred many a slave in the slave-holding American South to rebel, and some to escape. Contrary to the all-too-tidy and sanitized accounts of that sad era in American history, significant numbers of African American slaves rebelled against the wretchedness of their lot and sought blessed freedom by running away from the plantation. Runaway notices were common items in local newspapers in southern states, and the slave-holding class marshaled all available forces to hunt down and recapture those who had escaped their masters, and severe punishments ensued when escapees were apprehended. Few white Christian leaders in the South challenged that unjust and burdensome system, or aided those who sought freedom from that region's "peculiar institution."[1] As in Rome of old, slavery was such an entrenched system, so vital to the economy, and so backed by legal protections that most southerners, even confessed Christians, felt duty-bound to honor and defend slavery as proper and necessary.

No, Paul did not honor slavery as a good. No unjust system is ever good or proper and necessary. We should therefore not overlook the instruction to Christian slaves that Paul voiced in 1 Corinthians 7:21: "If you were a slave when you were called, don't let it bother [Greek, *meleto*, "worry"] you. But if you are actually able to be free, take advantage of the opportunity." Paul thought Onesimus worthy of that freedom and Paul used his influence in an appeal to Philemon to grant him that freedom. Paul felt convinced that Philemon would do so. "I'm writing to you, confident of your obedience and knowing that you will do more than what I ask" (verse 21). One wonders what "more than what I ask" would involve: a better status for other slaves in the household, once they were told about Philemon's release of Onesimus? We wonder, but cannot know.

Live the Story

As Christians we should embrace the message of Paul's Letter to Philemon that a shared faith should lead to transformed relationships. Social class and human differences are nullified in Christ, and they must yield to *agape*-love. Living as a Christian involves more than *faith* in Jesus as Savior and a steadying *hope* to receive what God has willed through him for us. A vital Christian life also includes being stirred by an aggressive *love* that bids us relate openly, honestly, humbly, and meaningfully with others, always seeking their good, and seeking forgiveness when we fail to do so.

Many will recall the well-publicized news of June 1995 that the Southern Baptist Convention, the largest Protestant denomination in the United States, at its annual meeting passed a resolution of repentance for the denomination's support of slavery, one of the contributing causes for founding their Convention in May, 1845, one hundred and fifty years earlier. A public apology was made to African Americans, whose ancestors suffered under the pernicious system of slavery. The Convention asked to be forgiven for justifying the slavery system, for its involvement in the systematic segregation that followed slavery, and for its part in helping shape the racist climate that still afflicts the nation. The Convention delegates eagerly sought reconciliation, and they made confession and sought forgiveness in order to experience this benefit. Their apology was responsibly made, based on an acknowledged "change of heart." The Spirit of God works steadily in every true believer to heighten our moral and social conscience and to encourage unselfish caring on our part.

Paul was right to applaud Philemon's characteristic "love and faithfulness" (verse 5) before voicing his appeal regarding Onesimus, because only love could inspire the openness needed both to be reconciled with Onesimus and to release him from his slave status. But *agape*-love can be trusted because it inspires caring and promotes the good of others! Paul used his influence to secure a needed benefit for Onesimus. Paul expressed the contagious principle that always motivated him when he advised believers: "So then, let's work for the good of all whenever we have an opportunity, and especially for those in the household of faith" (Galatians 6:10).

What might God be calling *your* congregation to do to overcome the legacy of racism in your community? What might God be calling *you* personally to do to use your voice and influence on behalf of someone suffering from injustice?

1. A euphemism for slavery and its ramifications in the American South, popular in the eighteenth and nineteenth centuries.

Leader Guide

People often view the Bible as a maze of obscure people, places, and events from centuries ago and struggle to relate it to their daily lives. IMMERSION invites us to experience the Bible as a record of God's loving revelation to humankind. These studies recognize our emotional, spiritual, and intellectual needs and welcome us into the Bible story and into deeper faith.

As leader of an IMMERSION group, you will help participants to encounter the Word of God and the God of the Word that will lead to new creation in Christ. You do not have to be an expert to lead; in fact, you will participate with your group in listening to and applying God's life-transforming Word to your lives. You and your group will explore the building blocks of the Christian faith through key stories, people, ideas, and teachings in every book of the Bible. You will also explore the bridges and points of connection between the Old and New Testaments.

Choosing and Using the Bible

The central goal of IMMERSION is engaging the members of your group with the Bible in a way that informs their minds, forms their hearts, and transforms the way they live out their Christian faith. Participants will need this study book and a Bible. IMMERSION is an excellent accompaniment to the Common English Bible (CEB). It shares with the CEB four common aims: clarity of language, faith in the Bible's power to transform lives, the emotional expectation that people will find the love of God, and the rational expectation that people will find the knowledge of God.

Other recommended study Bibles include *The New Interpreter's Study Bible* (NRSV), *The New Oxford Annotated Study Bible* (NRSV), *The HarperCollins Study Bible* (NRSV), the *NIV and TNIV Study Bibles*, and the *Archaeological Study Bible* (NIV). Encourage participants to use more than one translation. *The Message: The Bible in Contemporary Language* is a modern paraphrase of the Bible, based on the original languages. Eugene H. Peterson has created a masterful presentation of the Scripture text, which is best used alongside rather than in place of the CEB or another primary English translation.

One of the most reliable interpreters of the Bible's meaning is the Bible itself. Invite participants first of all to allow Scripture to have its say. Pay attention to context. Ask questions of the text. Read every passage with curiosity, always seeking to answer the basic Who? What? Where? When? and Why? questions.

Bible study groups should also have handy essential reference resources in case someone wants more information or needs clarification on specific words, terms, concepts, places, or people mentioned in the Bible. A Bible dictionary, Bible atlas, concordance, and one-volume Bible commentary together make for a good, basic reference library.

The Leader's Role

An effective leader prepares ahead. This leader guide provides easy-to-follow, step-by-step suggestions for leading a group. The key task of the leader is to guide discussion and activities that will engage heart and head and will invite faith development. Discussion questions are included, and you may want to add questions posed by you or your group. Here are suggestions for helping your group engage Scripture:

State questions clearly and simply.

Ask questions that move Bible truths from "outside" (dealing with concepts, ideas, or information about a passage) to "inside" (relating to the experiences, hopes, and dreams of the participants).

Work for variety in your questions, including compare and contrast, information recall, motivation, connections, speculation, and evaluation.

Avoid questions that call for yes-or-no responses or answers that are obvious.

Don't be afraid of silence during a discussion. It often yields especially thoughtful comments.

Test questions before using them by attempting to answer them yourself.

When leading a discussion, pay attention to the mood of your group by "listening" with your eyes as well as your ears.

Guidelines for the Group

IMMERSION is designed to promote full engagement with the Bible for the purpose of growing faith and building up Christian community. While much can be gained from individual reading, a group Bible study offers an ideal setting in which to achieve these aims. Encourage participants to bring their Bibles and read from Scripture during the session. Invite participants to consider the following guidelines as they participate in the group:

Respect differences of interpretation and understanding.

Support one another with Christian kindness, compassion, and courtesy.

Listen to others with the goal of understanding rather than agreeing or disagreeing.

Celebrate the opportunity to grow in faith through Bible study.

Approach the Bible as a dialogue partner, open to the possibility of being challenged or changed by God's Word.

Recognize that each person brings unique and valuable life experiences to the group and is an important part of the community.

Reflect theologically—that is, be attentive to three basic questions: What does this say about God? What does this say about me/us? What does this say about the relationship between God and me/us?

Commit to a lived faith response in light of insights you gain from the Bible. In other words, what changes in attitudes (how you believe) or actions (how you behave) are called for by God's Word?

Group Sessions

The group sessions, like the chapters themselves, are built around three sections: "Claim Your Story," "Enter the Bible Story," and "Live the Story." Sessions are designed to move participants from an awareness of their own life story, issues, needs, and experiences into an encounter and dialogue with the story of Scripture and to make decisions integrating their personal stories and the Bible's story.

The session plans in the following pages will provide questions and activities to help your group focus on the particular content of each chapter. In addition to questions and activities, the plans will include chapter title, Scripture, and faith focus.

Here are things to keep in mind for all the sessions:

Prepare Ahead

Study the Scripture, comparing different translations and perhaps a paraphrase.

Read the chapter, and consider what it says about your life and the Scripture.

Gather materials such as large sheets of paper or a markerboard with markers.

Prepare the learning area. Write the faith focus for all to see.

Welcome Participants

Invite participants to greet one another.

Tell them to find one or two people and talk about the faith focus.

Ask: What words stand out for you? Why?

Guide the Session

Look together at "Claim Your Story." Ask participants to give their reactions to the stories and examples given in each chapter. Use questions from the session plan to elicit comments based on personal experiences and insights.

Ask participants to open their Bibles and "Enter the Bible Story." For each portion of Scripture, use questions from the session plan to help participants gain insight into the text and relate it to issues in their own lives.

Step through the activity or questions posed in "Live the Story." Encourage participants to embrace what they have learned and to apply it in their daily lives.

Invite participants to offer their responses or insights about the boxed material in "Across the Testaments," "About the Scripture," and "About the Christian Faith."

Close the Session

Encourage participants to read the following week's Scripture and chapter before the next session.

Offer a closing prayer.

1. On Being Responsible
1 Timothy 1:1–3:16

Faith Focus

Christians are called to be faithful and responsible in teaching and learning, in prayer, and in action.

Before the Session

If you have not already done so, read the book of First Timothy. It would be helpful to have a map of Paul's missionary journeys to refer to. You will need large sheets of paper and felt-tipped markers.

Reflect on those leaders who mentored you in your younger years. How did their lives embody attention to doctrine, godliness, and devotion to duty?

Claim Your Story

Invite participants to share what chores they were assigned by their parents when they were young. What did they learn from doing these tasks? Did they view the jobs as busy work, or was there a sense of making a contribution to family life? What lessons were transferable to their adult lives?

Invite someone to briefly summarize what the study writer says was the reason for the writing of this letter. On a large sheet of paper, jot down the themes of the letter: trustworthiness, attentiveness to doctrine, godliness, and devotion to duty.

Enter the Bible Story

Timothy was one of Paul's closest associates in ministry. Ask volunteers to read the references to Timothy from other letters that the study writer cites, then have someone read aloud Acts 16:1-3. If you obtained a map of Paul's missionary journeys, point out the locations where Timothy accompanied Paul.

Refer the group members to the list of the letter's themes. Invite them to read 1 Timothy 1:3-10. Which of the letter's themes emerge here as Paul lays out Timothy's purpose in Ephesus?

Invite someone to read aloud Acts 7:54 –8:3; 9:1-2, the description of Saul's persecution of the Christians prior to his conversion. Then read aloud 1 Timothy

1:12-17, Paul's testimonial thanksgiving. In what ways had Paul experienced grace, mercy, love, and faith? How had his life been transformed? Have participants experienced a dramatic Damascus Road conversion, or something more gradual? How have their lives been shaped by grace, mercy, love, and faith?

Ask group members to name the categories of prayer that Paul includes and to briefly describe each category. How does the group respond to the instruction that congregational prayer should include prayer for the public order? The study writer suggests that prayer can influence the direction of civic decisions and that Christians should understand congregational prayer as a part of our Christian work in the world. What happens when we fail to include such prayers for the public good?

Invite participants to discuss how we can pray for and about issues that affect the public sector without resorting to partisan prayers or prayers directed at some group with political views that differ from ours. How do we pray in such a way that we allow room for the Spirit to work in and through us in these matters?

Ask group members to silently read Acts 19:23-41. Then ask one person to name the first detail in that account, with others adding additional details in order until a summary of the story is complete. The study writer suggests that this passage may shed some light on 1 Timothy 2:8-15. In what way? On a large sheet of paper, list 1 Timothy 2:8-15, Galatians 3:28, and 1 Corinthians 11:5. What picture of gender relations does each Scripture paint? How does the group reconcile these three statements of Paul? The study writer observes that the verses from Timothy are distinctly individual in tone and not intended as an absolute principle. How does the group respond? Invite them to suggest possible scenarios that might account for these instructions to Timothy.

Divide participants into two smaller groups. Give each a large sheet of paper and a felt-tipped marker. Ask one group to generate a list of the qualifications for "supervisors" in the church and the other a list for "servants." Then compare the two lists. What differences, if any, does the group notice? In considering the leadership of your congregation, do the two lists apply to what we look for in a leader? What other qualities might we add?

Live the Story

The study writer lifts up the importance of the concept of responsibility, seeing it as central to our self-understanding and fulfillment. As persons created to be responsible, what does it mean that at our conversion we are recreated in Christ to act with accountability to the truth as it reveals itself in Jesus? What guides us as we seek to witness and to share ourselves in service to God and neighbor? How in our lives do we demonstrate that we, like Timothy are true children in the faith?

Close by reading 1 Timothy 1:15-16 aloud, and then have everyone read verse 17 aloud as a benediction.

2. Maintaining Community Order
1 Timothy 4:1–6:21

Faith Focus

As leaders and members of the church, we are charged with embodying, protecting, and passing on the gospel message.

Before the Session

On a large sheet of paper, print the prompt: "To me, the church is . . ." Head another sheet with the words "Signs of Life and Vitality in the Church." Obtain paper and pencils or pens for participants.

Claim Your Story

Call the group's attention to the prompt about the church. Ask them to respond out loud, popcorn style, with the first thing that comes to mind when they think of the church. Print their responses on the sheet. Consider some of the questions the study writer raises in the first paragraph of the study (page 19), and invite participants to reflect more deeply on the question of how to define *church*. Encourage them to name signs of life and vitality in your congregation, and if applicable, your denomination, and list these on the sheet. What in their opinion are the most important indicators of vitality? Growth in numbers? Indications of a commitment to mission, justice, or evangelism? Something else? With what indicators does First Timothy equate church vitality?

Enter the Bible Story

On a large sheet of paper or a markerboard, print "Positive Happenings." Ask participants to list those happenings that serve to motivate a desire for clarified thinking, increased understanding, and disciplined living in church members. Print "Negative Happenings" on another sheet of paper or the board, and ask: What are some events that block rather than bless the church's mission? What are some indicators that people who are still in the faith community have nonetheless turned away from the faith? When and in what ways would it be possible for an ascetic lifestyle to actually block the full development of faith? Invite someone to read aloud Genesis 1:1–2:4a. How does the affirmation that God's creation is very good make a practical difference in our attitudes and behavior regarding the gift of food or the gift of sexuality?

Ask group members to name the spiritual practices Paul names that will provide Timothy with help in training himself in godliness (see 1 Timothy 4:7b-16). How do these practices bear fruit for leaders in the church today? Call the group's attention to the section in the study about elders (page 23). What does Paul have to say about choosing leaders in the church? How do we today approach the task of appointing, commissioning, and installing our leadership? Is there room in the way we choose and nurture leaders for younger as well as more mature leadership? What role does discernment play? If we find that a leader is exhibiting troubling behavior, how does the church address it?

Invite participants to select one of the following topics and form small groups for discussion: care for widows and orphans, generational issues, slaves, and moneyed members. If you find that no one is opting for one of the topics, plan to discuss it briefly in the larger group. Encourage the groups to read the Scripture verses and the material in the study and try to address the following: what Paul is saying about this topic; what we would say about it today; what questions the small group has; how we believe God is speaking to us at this moment about this topic. In the total group, invite participants to share their thoughts. Are all of these topics relevant to our lives as Christians today? In what ways? What about the topic of slavery? Where are the parallels today? Are there systems of injustice and oppression today that we tacitly accept, as Paul seems to accept slavery?

Live the Story

Ask participants to revisit their responses to the open-ended statement about the church and what it is to them. The study writer observes that the intricate mosaic of persons that is the church must be considered as more than a voluntary association or a club. Which of their responses are consistent with the understanding that the church is God's household, called by God into a community of faith? Do some responses lean more toward a view of the church as a voluntary association, a social club, or a place to make business contacts? Do some reflect a view of the church as a place to go, rather than a community from which to be sent in discipleship into the world? How does this understanding of the church shape the way we view, choose, and carry out leadership roles? How does this congregation live out, preserve, and pass on the faith?

Distribute paper and pencils or pens and invite participants to reflect on and respond in writing to the questions in the final paragraph of the study (pages 27–28). After several minutes, invite participants to share aloud some of their responses to those questions. Encourage them to revisit these questions and their responses as a part of their devotional time in the coming days.

Close with your own prayer or with the following:

"O gracious God, we pray for your holy Church universal,
    that you would be pleased to fill it with all truth, in all peace.
Where it is corrupt, purify it;
where it is in error, direct it;
where in any thing it is amiss, reform it;
where it is right, establish it;
where it is in want, provide for it;
where it is divided, reunite it;
for the sake of him who died and rose again,
    and ever lives to make intercession for us,
    Jesus Christ, your Son, our Lord. Amen."[1]

---

1. From *The Book of Common Prayer*, in *The United Methodist Book of Worship* (Copyright © 1992 by The United Methodist Publishing House), 501.

3. We Do Not Walk Alone
2 Timothy 1:1–2:26

Faith Focus

Christians find encouragement and peace of mind, even in the midst of trials and tribulations, when we remember that God is with us.

Before the Session

Post a large sheet of paper headed "Who is it that walks with you?" Obtain some colored self-stick notes and pens or pencils for participants. Gather a variety of kinds of bowls or vessels—wooden, silver, ceramic, pottery, even plastic or paper. If you decide to use the hymn "Nothing Between My Soul and My Savior," locate it in a hymnal or download the lyrics from the Internet (on some sites the music can also be played).

Claim Your Story

As participants arrive, invite them to read the anecdote about Oprah Winfrey on page 29. Then ask them to consider who walks with them. It may be persons in their own family tree, or it could be others who have served as mentors to them. For some, it may be a prominent historical or political figure. Ask them to think about whose example they consider when they have a decision to make. Invite them to print one or more names on self-stick notes and attach them to the large sheet of paper. As each person attaches a note, invite him or her to speak to two questions: How has this person influenced you? Do you have an actual sense of the person's presence in times when you are in need of discernment?

Enter the Bible Story

In Paul's first letter to Timothy, he reveals the close relationship the two had. Ask group members to try to imagine being Timothy, a young disciple who receives a letter from his mentor, Paul, who is in prison. Invite a volunteer to read aloud 2 Timothy 1:1-18. What indications do group members hear in this portion of the letter of that relationship? Where do they hear encouragement? Advice? Invite them to share how they might have been feeling had they been Timothy. What were the duties he needed to fulfill?

In that time Christianity had yet to become respectable, and a life lived in accord with the will of God inevitably placed the believer in conflict with evil in the world. What about in our context, when Christianity is the essence of respectability? Do we ever find ourselves at odds with the popularized image of what it means to be a Christian, especially when the portrayal of our faith is sometimes more like a caricature? Ask participants if they have ever been faced with the choice of being stigmatized for their actions, as did Onesiphorus in visiting Paul in prison. In our own society, what kinds of actions or stands might a Christian choose that would have stigmatizing consequences?

Ask someone to read aloud the sidebar about Paul's admiration for the image of the soldier (page 34). Give participants a few minutes to think about a role in today's society that appeals to them. What qualities or features of that role could be used to compare how we might engage in following Jesus?

Divide the group into three smaller groups or pairs, and assign to each group one of the three instructions Paul gives to Timothy about how to remain an approved worker in God's church (page 35). Ask them to discuss what they would say about this piece of advice to a young person who is assuming a leadership role in the church. How does this advice apply to participants who are older leaders in the church? Are there particular pitfalls associated with either younger or more mature leaders?

If you brought a variety of vessels or bowls, invite the group to examine them. What sort of "vessel" do members of the group imagine themselves to be? Invite them to come up and examine the bowls or containers you gathered and to choose one they might compare themselves to. Ask volunteers to tell why they identified with the vessel they chose. For what special purpose do they imagine they have been formed in this way?

Live the Story

Paul's instructions to Timothy in this letter suggest that the younger man had run up against obstacles blocking him from doing what he was sent to Ephesus to do. Distribute paper and pencils or pens. Ask participants to draw a wall or obstacle on the page and to imagine it represents what is blocking them from fully living out their discipleship. Invite them to write words or phrases that represent the feelings, problems, persons, events, or circumstances that represent that blockage. Consider together the questions posed by the study writer. What, if any, injuries have group members sustained in their service to the Lord? In what ways have injuries and conflicts shaped them? How have they felt God's presence?

Close by singing or reading the lyrics of the hymn "Nothing Between My Soul and My Savior."

4. The Comfort and the Counsel That Sustain Us

2 Timothy 3:1–4:22

Faith Focus

Christians are not immune from the distress, hurt, fears, and suffering that life brings. But we find comfort and strength in Scripture and in the love that others have shown us.

Before the Session

On a large sheet of paper, print the following: "Understand that the last days will be dangerous times . . ." You will need paper and pencils or pens for participants. If possible, have available a map of Paul's missionary journeys.

Claim Your Story

Invite participants to read the story about how Howard Thurman's grandmother's presence and counsel helped Thurman and his siblings face the difficulties of life in segregated Daytona Beach (page 40). Distribute paper and pens or pencils. Ask them to jot down the name of a person from their childhood who grounded them in a similar fashion—a parent, grandparent, or some other person. Ask them to write down a difficult experience or incident they faced as a child and finally a phrase or sentence about how that person helped them. Invite those who are willing to share what they wrote. Calling to mind such personal experiences can help the group members better understand the role of Paul in Timothy's life.

Enter the Bible Story

Invite a volunteer to read aloud 2 Timothy 3:1-9, Paul's warning to Timothy that difficult times are ahead. Look together at the sheet of paper you posted. Remind the participants that Paul, like most of the early church, expected Jesus to return very soon. These verses read like a current news account. Invite them to name aspects of our current context that mirror what Paul is saying, and print these on the sheet. Is there evidence that the church today, at least in the Western context, is suffering as people violently oppose the truth? Might there be more subtle dangers threatening the church in our postmodern context? Are there modern equivalents of the Egyptian magicians Jannes and Jambres, persons or groups who use smoke and mirrors to threaten the church?

If you have a map, ask volunteers to locate and point out the places where Paul faced difficulties. Paul reminds Timothy that anyone who lives a holy life will be harassed, encouraging Timothy to live by the Scriptures so that he will be equipped for doing good. In what circumstances today have participants experienced people who would rather listen to those whose message pleases them? Are there those today who yearn for myths rather than the values that lead to godliness? How do we answer those who say that God rewards them with wealth or influence?

Invite someone to read the passage from Philippians quoted in the study (under "Paul Anticipates His Final Transition," page 43) where Paul shares his secret for coping well with trouble and transition. Discuss what Paul says in Romans, that he is confident that God is in control and will work for good in all situations. How does the group react to that?

Invite group members to imagine that Timothy was able to heed Paul's entreaties to come to him before November when regular ship travel on the Mediterranean closed down. The study writer observes that Timothy later experienced being imprisoned himself. What might he have learned from Paul about how to endure such an experience? What might Timothy have told others about this visit with his beloved friend?

Invite volunteers to share times in their lives when they may have endured painful transitions and difficult times. Where did they find comfort and hope? In Scripture? In the ministry of family and friends? If they could share with a younger person what they have learned from these times, what would they say?

Paul does not view his approaching death as a sad ending, but as a transition to a new beginning. How do participants view death? Are they apprehensive? Does the idea of death suggest an ultimate fulfillment? Do we have an expectation of good?

Live the Story

Ask the group to consider in silence the ways they are in transition. What circumstances, situations, or relationships leave them feeling imprisoned? In the face of these things, how can they strengthen their faith and trust in God? What wisdom and guidance can they find in Scripture, and to which Scriptures would they turn?

As the study writer suggests, invite participants to recall the persons whose presence and counsel helped them get through troubles and transition. Invite them to name these people out loud. Pray for all these people, living and dead, who represent a "cloud of witnesses" for participants. Distribute paper and pens or pencils and encourage participants to write a short note to those persons still living who had this kind of influence in their lives.

Close by reading aloud the two stanzas from "A Charge to Keep I Have" or sing them together.

5. Living Faithfully in a Hostile Environment
Paul's Letter to Titus

Faith Focus

We can live holy lives even in hostile environments because God's grace forgives us, shapes us, and empowers us.

Before the Session

On a large sheet of paper, print the words "Who?" "What?" "When?" "Where?" and "Why?" down the left margin, leaving space in between for writing. Get copies of your denominational hymnal. If the hymns "Amazing Grace," "I Am Thine, O Lord," and "Grace Greater than Our Sin" are not there, download the lyrics from the Internet and make copies.

Claim Your Story

Invite participants to share situations where they experienced hostility. Did that hostility seem to stem from differences in race, class, ideology, or values? How did participants respond to the circumstances in which they found themselves? Did they react with hostility in kind? Remain silent or retreat from the situation? If the hostility was aimed at their Christian values, were they able to hold fast to what they believed or how they knew they should respond? Did they experience an internal struggle over maintaining their values? Does it make a difference if hostility is short term or a long term situation in which one must live? Ask participants to silently read over the questions posed by the study writer (pages 49-50). In this Letter to Titus, Paul struggles with these same issues.

Enter the Bible Story

Ask someone to read the greeting that opens the Book of Titus (verses 1-3), and invite volunteers to summarize the themes of the letter revealed there. On a large sheet of paper, print the words "faith," "knowledge of the truth," "godliness," "hope," and "eternal life."

Call attention to the sheet with the questions "Who? What? When? and Where?" Depending on the size of your group, assign one question to two or three people. Ask them to read the relevant information under "Concerning Titus the Man" and "Titus's Pastoral Task on Crete" (pages 50-51), as well as any pertinent Scriptures. Then have each group report briefly as you print a line or two under the relevant question. If you have a map of Paul's missionary journeys, the group assigned "Where?" can point out where Crete is located with respect to Paul's travels. Together, answer the "Why?" question: Why was Titus where he was?

Churches do not exist in a vacuum but rather are part of some larger societal setting. What was the threat represented by the religious opposition of the Jews? Ask the group to quickly scan Acts 15:1-35. Why were Jewish members insisting on circumcision of male Gentiles? How was the issue resolved? Are there "litmus test" issues today that some Christians insist are essential for salvation? Do any of these represent a threat in your congregation's context?

The study writer observes that for Paul, faith and knowledge of the truth have the intended goal of producing godliness. How does Paul define godliness? Ask someone to read aloud Titus 2:1-10. How does the group respond to this description of how members of the household are to relate? Is anything problematic or troubling? Earlier in the letter, Paul connects the behavior of children in a household with the qualifications of a person to serve as a leader in the church. Does the group agree with this criterion? Why or why not?

Ask participants to respond with a show of hands if they agree that Paul's position on slavery is justified, given the environment in which he lived. Ask those who agree to describe why they agree with Paul's position as revealed in Titus and other letters. Then ask those who disagree to explain why. Paul wants believers to behave in their households in ways that draw approval and respect of outsiders. Is there ever a time when a believer must take a stand that may not bring the approval of the larger society?

Divide the group into three smaller groups or pairs. Assign to each group one of the following hymns: "Amazing Grace," "I Am Thine, O Lord," and "Grace Greater than Our Sin." Ask them to read over the lyrics, along with the information in the study about grace (pages 54-55). If time allows, they can also check the subject index of the hymnal and read over other lyrics about grace.

Discuss together what the hymns reveal about God's grace. How is God's grace justifying? Sanctifying? What does it mean that the salvation brought by God's grace enables us to live *in* the world, but not *like* the world?

Live the Story

Review the question of *why* Titus was in Crete. The writer tells us that his reason for being there was not *casual*, but *causal*—the cause of the gospel. Encourage participants to reflect on their own mission—the why of their lives as Christians saved by grace. Use Fanny Crosby's words as a closing prayer.

6. Using Influence Unselfishly
Paul's Letter to Philemon

Faith Focus

Christ's love persuades us to act with mercy, forgiveness, and a desire for unity and the well-being of all.

Before the Session

In advance of the session, contact a person who is an expressive reader and ask him or her to be prepared to read Philemon aloud to the group. You will need a large sheet of paper and a felt-tipped marker.

Claim Your Story

Invite participants to consider the layers of social stratification in your community. Ask them to name the groups that constitute the "upper crust," and print these names at the top of a large sheet of paper. Then ask them to suggest who is on the bottom in your environment, and print these at the bottom of the sheet. What groups range from that top layer to the bottom? Why do they think certain groups are placed where they are? Have they ever been guilty of labeling someone as just poor, or wealthy, or an immigrant, or a person of color, without considering that each person is far more than just a socially determined category? Where do they themselves fall in this social layer cake? The Letter to Philemon calls us to revisit what it can mean to someone low in the social system to be seen, understood, and treated as a person of worth and dignity.

Enter the Bible Story

Ask group members to name the two possible reasons suggested by the study writer that this letter was included in the New Testament. Today, its importance may be to shed light on what it means to be fellow members of the body of Christ. Because the Letter to Philemon is so short, invite the group to listen as someone reads it aloud in its entirety. Suggest that as they listen, they picture themselves as a member of Philemon's household who is hearing the letter read—perhaps a member of the house church that met in Philemon's house, or perhaps one of the household slaves. How would the letter be heard by these persons? What does the letter say about the character of Philemon?

Divide the group into two smaller groups, and allow participants to choose between two topics: (1) What about slavery and the case for Paul's position? and (2) What do we know about Onesimus? Ask the groups to read the information in the study and in the letter itself and be prepared to present the evidence they find. Allow about five minutes for them to work. Then ask each group to present what it has found. What questions remain unanswered—about slavery, about where Paul stood on the issue, about just who Onesimus was and what he had done? With the evidence in this letter and in previous ones in this study, does the group consider Paul's position and approach to the issue of systemic slavery justified? Why or why not? How does the way Paul portrays Onesimus's usefulness transcend the social category of slavery? In the group's opinion, is it likely that Philemon released Onesimus? What did Paul mean when he asked Philemon to do more than he asked? Is he asking for improved status for other slaves in the household? The release of those slaves, too? A transcending of socially constricting roles so that those slaves are viewed as brothers and sisters?

Review together the information in the study about the American institution of slavery (pages 64–65). Why did Christians of the time honor and defend slavery? What happens when an unjust system becomes entrenched because of its perceived economic necessity? Some would say our approach to immigration issues is a breeding ground for injustices. Are undocumented persons potentially victimized by unjust systems? What would happen if we viewed them as brothers and sisters in Christ? What could we do to overcome not just the legacy of racism, which is still stubbornly entrenched in our culture, but other systemic injustices that impact the lives of those who live on the margins?

Live the Story

As Christians we should embrace the message of this letter that a shared faith should lead to transformed relationships where social class and human prejudices are nullified. More than just faith and hope, as important as these are, Christian living involves being stirred by an aggressive love. What, in the participants' opinion, are the characteristics of *agape*-love?

Ask participants to consider again the sheet of paper where you recorded the social layer cake that is your community. What might God be calling your congregation—and you personally—to do to demonstrate *agape*-love and to work for the good of all? Say a closing prayer asking God to move you toward living the kind of love that leads to transformed relationships that touch every strata of society.